LOCAL HEROES

An Epic WW2 Shipwreck and Survival Story

Neil Carlsen

FUTURES PUBLICATIONS

Copyright © 2010 Neil Carlsen

Published by

FUTURES PUBLICATIONS

www.futurespublications.co.uk

First published in March 2010

ISBN: 978-1-871131-19-2

Contact the Author: *neil.carlsen@omega.no*

Cover design and layout by Torbjørn Vik Lunde: *torbjornlunde@me.com*

Edited by Vincent P. Bartley: *vpb@subtext.no*

Cover Photos:

Front: (left to right):
Edward Briggs Hyde, Apprentice, Cullercoats
(Isabel McGregor - Private Collection)
James Nicholson Meeks, Apprentice, South Shields (National Archives)
John Albert Morley, Able Seaman, Hull (National Archives)
SS Peterton (John H. Marsh Maritime Collection, Cape Town, South Africa)

Back Page: (from top):
Thomas Cuthbert Gorman, Chief Engineer, Hull (National Archives)
George Denis Howes, Second Officer, Hull (National Archives)
U-109 (Bundesarchiv)

All rights reserved. No part of the contents of this book may be reproduced or transmitted in any form or by any means, including recording or any information storage and retrieval system without written permission from the publisher.

Printed in the United Kingdom by Tandem Press
www.tandempress.com

CONTENTS

1. Introduction 5
2. Boys and Boats 15
3. Hunter and Hunted 32
4. The Attack 57
5. Lifeboat Voyage 75
6. Freetown, Sierra Leone 128
7. Local Heroes 147
8. The Sinking of U-109 and the End of the U-boat War 156
9. The War Goes On: 1943 – 1945 169
10. Return to Freetown – The Post War Years 197
11. Appendix I. War Service Record – James Nicholson Meeks . . 209
12. Appendix II. List of the Crew: SS Peterton 216
13. Appendix III. List of the Crew: U-109 222
14. Appendix IV. Technical Information for U-109 Type IXB 225
15. Appendix V. Gallantry Awards during the Second World War (Merchant Navy) 226
16. References 229
17. Acknowledgements 236

In Memory of
James Nicholson Meeks
and Edward Briggs Hyde

1

INTRODUCTION

'He's coming up just right,' I heard Bleichrodt say. 'He has two guns astern by the look of it and several Oerlikons.' Two hours after we had first sighted the ship we fired three torpedoes at a range of 800 yards and hit her with all three. She immediately assumed a heavy list to port, got her boats away, capsized and went down by the bows.

Radio Officer Wolfgang Hirschfeld describes the last moments of SS *Peterton*, sunk by German U-boat U-109 on the 17th September 1942. Thirty-four survivors found themselves in two lifeboats, one containing Chief Officer Francis Buller Fairweather and eleven men, the other: 2nd Officer George Denis Howes and twenty-one men, including two fifteen-year-old boys on their first voyage, James 'Jimmy' Nicholson Meeks of South Shields and Edward 'Teddy' Briggs Hyde of Cullercoats. One of the boats was about to embark on one of the epic lifeboat voyages of World War Two.

Bringing this story to a wider audience has been the result of the author's own personal voyage, a voyage of discovery, and one which, like the crew of the *Peterton*, turned out to be much longer than expected. My own journey began nearly thirty years ago when my mother handed me a scrap from a war-era newspaper which reported a remarkable 49 day voyage in an open lifeboat endured by her brother, James Nicholson Meeks, who was a fifteen-year-old at the time, an even younger fellow-apprentice and a group of survivors. The article, dated January 1943, had been torn from a local newspaper, *The Shields Gazette*, and laid forgotten in the bottom of a bedroom drawer for years. Much of it had been censored and aside from mentioning the sinking of a ship and a lifeboat voyage, there was precious little detail other than a few words on water supplies and how the survivors from the shipwreck passed their time. Despite its brevity, I was intrigued by the story. It sounded like something from a Boys Own annual. Having said that, I doubted I would have had the bottle to join the Merchant Navy as a fifteen-year-old in the middle of a world war, away from all my mates and family. As for surviving 49 days in an open lifeboat in the middle of the Atlantic Ocean with barely any food or water, that was beyond the powers of even my over-active imagination.

There would be plenty of time to reflect on these questions for twenty years would pass before Jimmy's story came to my attention again. His widow, Peggy (née Hargreaves), was telling me one day about her husband's life in the Merchant Navy when, quite unexpectedly, she produced a copy of the very same newspaper cutting my mother had shown me all those years before. My interest in the story was rekindled but another six years would pass before interest turned into action. Late one evening in the summer of 2001, I tuned into a documentary on National Geographic Channel. The documentary had been produced by a team of American divers who had discovered a previously uncharted wreck of a German U-boat off the east coast of the United States. Their five-year endeavour to identify the U-boat (U-869), previously believed to have been lost in the approaches to Gibraltar, and the documentary's moving conclusion, inspired me to embark on the story of the sinking of the *Peterton* and the survivors' incredible lifeboat voyage.

A major obstacle facing me when setting out on this project was that the one person who could provide most of the information, Jimmy Meeks, was no longer with us. I had to start my research somewhere and my first port of call was to the person closest to both of us: my mother, Margaret Meeks, who was Jimmy's youngest sister. Unfortunately, she did not remember the name of the ship. The newspaper cutting was missing too, which was a set-back. I called Jimmy Meeks' daughters: Lynda and Janice, firstly to obtain their approval for the project and then to ask if they could remember the name of their father's ship. Unfortunately, neither of them could remember this key piece of information. However, I did learn that Peggy Meeks' copy of the newspaper cutting was now in the possession of youngest daughter, Janice. She promised to dig it out and fax a copy to me later.

In the meantime, I widened my search by accessing the National Archives website and its on-line database, The Catalogue. Here, it was explained that a discharge number was the key to locating the service records of Merchant Navy seamen and that individual records are contained in document files known as Seamen's' Pouches. The Catalogue contains references for all merchant seamen who served between 1912 and 1972. Entering the name 'Meeks' and his birthplace 'South Shields' revealed the first surprise, no less than seven members of the Meeks family from South Shields had served in the merchant navy since 1912. One of the names listed, was a James Meeks R285651 born on the 7th October 1926. I called his elder daughter, Lynda, the same evening and she confirmed this was her father's date of birth; Merchant Navy

Seaman R285651 was the James Meeks I was looking for. Crucially, Lynda also remembered the name of the apprentice who sailed with Jimmy in the lifeboat. His name was Edward Briggs Hyde.

Having confirmed Jimmy Meeks' discharge number, the next step was to manually access his file at the National Archives. I assigned this task to a local researcher who was familiar with the process. The same researcher informed me that if Jimmy's file contained the name of his torpedoed ship it may lead to a Shipping Casualty Report – an interview with the most senior ranking survivor.

Since this process was expected to take several days, I continued the detective work and rang Janice, again. I needed that newspaper cutting as my mother had failed to find the original. On speaking to her, I was told she had found the newspaper cutting taken from the *Shields Gazette* and, as an unexpected bonus, a letter of Commendation For Brave Conduct signed by Winston Churchill for 'James Nicholson Meeks'. Janice faxed them through to me the following day. The newspaper article confirmed the survivors had spent 49 days in an open lifeboat but no mention of the ship's name. However, the letter of commendation signed by Winston Churchill *did* include the name of the ship: *SS Peterton*.

I immediately contacted the National Archives researcher with this information and asked to concentrate his search on the *Peterton*. Now that I knew the name of the ship, it was a simple matter of determining from sources freely available online that the *Peterton* had been sunk by German U-boat U-109 on the 17th September 1942. This fact is also confirmed in definitive historical publications such as Jürgen Rohwer's U-boat directory: Axis Submarine Successes of World War Two.

As far as this account is concerned, the discovery that U-109 is the perpetrator of the sinking of the *Peterton* is an incredible stroke of luck since U-109's war exploits are well known following the publication of a book by Wolfgang Hirschfeld called Secret Diary of a U-boat. There are precious few first-hand accounts written by German submariners. This is entirely due to the appalling losses suffered by the German U-boat flotilla, less than 10,000 of the 40,000 submariners who served in German U-boats survived the war. Radio Officer Wolfgang Hirschfeld was one of the lucky few who survived the war. U-109's sympathetic radioman, ignored the spectre of a court martial by keeping a secret diary on each of his six patrols onboard U-109. These diaries formed the basis of his book. This remarkable account contains an insight into the sinking of the *Peterton* from the perspective of the U-boat and is recommended reading for anyone wishing to learn more about the lives of German submariners in World War Two.

Shortly after discovering that U-109 had sent the *Peterton* to the bottom of the Atlantic, word came from the National Archives that Jimmy Meeks' service records had been located and a 'very good' Shipping Casualty Report for the *Peterton*. The documents that arrived several days later were far better than I had hoped for, with service records containing period photographs, fingerprints and a Shipping Casualty Report every bit as good as promised. The details of the sinking, the survivors' rendezvous with U-109, which they thought was an Italian submarine, the capture of its master, Captain Thomas William Marrie (Sunderland) and their 49 day lifeboat ordeal are graphically described by 2nd Officer George Howes. The report also revealed that the *Peterton*'s survivors sailed in, not one, but two lifeboats.

Satisfied that the main pieces of the story were in my possession, I took a pause in my research. Up until this point I had made no plans to turn the story into a book and simply sent the results of my research to Jimmy Meeks' family. At the start of 2004, I picked up my research file again and realised that, with a bit more work, I could bring the story to a wider audience. The next phase of the project began with the sourcing of photographs. I wrote to the German U-boat archive in Cuxhaven in Northern Germany to ask them whether they had any further photographs relating to their sixth mission and in particular the sinking of the *Peterton*. I received a prompt and polite reply from U-boat veteran and U-Boote Archiv founder and director Horst Bredow, he was disappointed that he was unable to find more photos for me. He also mentioned that he was a good friend of Wolfgang Hirchsfeld and remained in regular contact with him.

A photograph of the *Peterton* was acquired through a chance encounter with American, Ken Dunn, of Charlotte, North Carolina USA. Ken is one of many U-boat enthusiasts around the world and possesses a wealth of literature and knowledge on the subject.

Photographs of Jimmy Meeks were easy to obtain from members his immediate family but since 2nd Officer George Denis Howes and Edward Briggs Hyde are central figures in this story, I was determined to source some photos of them too, so it was back to the National Archives again. This resulted in the acquisition of a photograph of 2nd Officer George Howes. I was disappointed to learn that no photographs existed of Edward Briggs Hyde but this was tempered by the acquisition of Jimmy Meeks' service record and Ship Movement record for the entire war and the List of

Crew from the *Peterton*'s last voyage. The crew list was important, not only for identifying the names of the *Peterton*'s crew, but also for confirming that Jimmy Meeks and Edward Briggs Hyde were actually onboard at the time of its loss.

In a last ditch attempt to find a photo of Edward Briggs Hyde, I rang his old Primary School in Cullercoats. School Secretary, Hilary Reynolds, found his record in the school's archive but did not have any photographs from that period. However, on her suggestion, I contacted local historian Peter Burns, who had written a book about the history of Cullercoats. I sent an email to Peter the following day. He immediately promised to help. The next day, a newspaper article from 1943, containing a report on Edward Hyde, arrived in my computer's inbox. The article revealed that Edward had two sisters and a brother who had served in the RAF. Peter Burns informed me that a friend knew where one of Edward's sisters lived and would write to her on my behalf. A week later an email arrived from Peter McGregor, Edward Hyde's nephew. He gave me his mother's number and said she was willing to talk about her late brother. Edward Hyde's sister, Isabel, informed me that her husband, Ken, had done his own research into her brother, Teddy's, dramatic lifeboat voyage. More importantly, they had photographs of him and also some wartime correspondence. With photographs of most the story's central characters in place, I began to focus my attention on locating survivors.

Of the twenty-two survivors in Jimmy Meeks' and Teddy Hyde's lifeboat, I figured that some of them may still be alive; though most would be in their eighties or nineties. Attempts at locating survivors by posting messages on Internet forums had drawn a blank. I was forced to resort to much cruder methods. I sat down with the List of Crew obtained from the National Archives and made a list of the youngest survivors and then searched for their phone numbers online. This produced a shortlist of only two names, one of whom was J. A. Morley of Hull. I called his number and the phone was answered by a lady whom I took to be Morley's wife. I asked her if anyone in the household had served in the Merchant Navy during the Second World War. When she told me her husband, Jack, had sailed during the war and had been torpedoed, I could barely believe my good fortune. 'It must be him!' I thought.

'Can I speak to him?'

'I'm sorry that won't be possible'.

My heart sank and, barely hiding my disappointment, I asked:

'Has he passed away?'

'No, he's out buying a lottery ticket!'

I was mightily relieved and not a little embarrassed by my ill-timed remark but Jack's wife took it all in her stride. She politely asked me to call back later but, before I had a chance to hang up, Jack was already returning from his brief errand. It felt like winning a lottery of my own when I heard Jack's voice for the first time. We spoke at length about his memory of events surrounding the sinking of the *Peterton*. His first hand testimony of its loss and his subsequent lifeboat voyage was grippingly enthralling. One of the most astonishing facts to emerge that day was that Jack had absolutely no idea that the *Peterton* had been sunk by a German U-boat. He had believed for over sixty years it had been sunk by an Italian submarine! I sincerely hoped he had not held a grudge against the Italians!

I returned to the National Archives again late in 2004. A local researcher provided me with several documents I had not seen before – A memorandum entitled: SURVIVORS FROM *"PETERTON"* written by Lt. Bishop-Laggett, the commander of *HMT Canna*, who picked up the *Peterton*'s starboard lifeboat, a questionnaire completed by a Naval Control Service Officer during an interview with 2nd Officer George Howes and several telegrams sent by British Authorities in Freetown and Buenos Aires, listing the names of ex-*Peterton* survivors picked up. In December 2009, I made a personal visit to the National Archives to search for photographs of the rest of the *Peterton*'s crew. There, I was able to find photographs of around half of the men, they are all included in this edition.

The result of almost ten years of research is this book, which includes a diary of the sinking of the *Peterton*, its historical timing in the Battle of the Atlantic and some comparative analysis with survival stories by other Merchant Navy seamen, biographies of James Nicholson Meeks, Edward Briggs Hyde and other members of the *Peterton*'s crew as well as background information on U-109 and its commander, Heinrich Bleichrodt. Bleichrodt ended the war as the German Kriegmarine's tenth most successful U-boat commander, sinking twenty seven ships at a total of 158,000 tons.

This work contains many voices, gathered from written and spoken testimonies by Merchant Navy veterans, Jimmy and Teddy's friends and family and, not least from my own experiences; I spent a lot of time with Jimmy Meeks, during my youth and knew him well. I am satisfied that this incredible story has now been presented in all its factual detail and hope it will inspire and continue to fascinate readers for many years to come. During the course of my research I was fortunate enough to contact many Merchant Navy veterans and enthusiasts like Jack Baron and Billy McGee and families of victims such as the McGregors, I am indebted to them all for their help.

When setting out on this story, Jimmy Meeks was the only local hero I had in mind, I had no idea so many others would emerge and how deserving they were of their decorations and commendations. So, this story is no longer just a story about my uncle, it is about all forty-two members of the crew of the *Peterton*.

2

BOYS AND BOATS

James Nicholson Meeks (inset) was born at his family home in South Shields on the 7th October 1926. His safe arrival came as a relief for parents, John Watson Meeks (1901–1961) and Margaret Grieve Meeks (née Christie) (1901–1982), who had lost their first child at birth the previous year. John Meeks already had one child from a previous marriage: a daughter called Georgina (Ena), (1921-1995).

The Meeks family had lived in South Shields since the early 1850's when Jimmy's great great-grandfather, Peter Meeks (c.1798–1857), moved there from his native Ireland. Peter and his wife Rose (née Naughton) (1798–1862) were Catholics and came from a village called Milltown, in the county of Westmeath, one hundred miles west of Dublin. Their departure from Ireland coincided with the national disaster that was the great potato famine of 1845–1850.

Family tradition has it that Peter and Rose Meeks produced twenty-one children and that all but one of them lived into adulthood. As unlikely as this may seem, census reports from the 1800s confirm that they arrived in South Shields with eight of their children: Thomas, Rose, Christopher, Bridget, Peter, Patrick, William and Annie. Thomas Meeks was the oldest and was born in 1825 when his mother was 27 years old, so it is likely she had had several children before then. Irish baptism records revealed that their second youngest child, Bernard (b. 1840), did not travel to South Shields with the rest of the family. The true number of Meeks children may not have been twenty-one but is likely to have been well into double figures.

Oldest boy, Thomas (b. 1825), and his Derry born wife, Jane (née Connoly), settled in Corstorphine Street in the Tyne Dock area, whilst the rest of the family lived under one roof in a house in East Adelaide Street, High Shields. Once the children began to marry and have children of their own they moved out, but did not go far. Christopher and Peter moved to a house in the neighbouring Cambridge Street, where they lived under one roof with their wives and children. Jimmy's great grandfather, Peter (1832–1893), had married local girl Mary Jane Watson (1839–1898) in 1856. Like many Irish immigrants of the time, Peter Meeks was illiterate; his marriage certificate of 1856 was signed only with a cross.

When the Meeks family first arrived in South Shields in the 1860s, the town's ship building industry was booming, and building and repair yards were in abundance. This had not always been the case. The monopoly held by the city of Newcastle had not been broken until 1720 when Robert Wallis opened a small shipyard in South Shields and won the legal actions launched against him by the Newcastle based shipyards. Despite the abundance of shipyards and their associated roperies and timber works, many of the males in the Meeks family found work in Tyne Dock's alkali works. The chemical industry in South Shields had developed on the back of the town's glass industry and a large demand for Alum in the production of blown, plate and flint glass. One of South

Shields' finest glassworks was owned by Cookson and Co. in Mill Dam and by the middle of the 19th century it was the largest in Britain, producing half of the plate glass used in the construction of the Crystal Palace.

By 1871, Peter and his wife, Mary Jane, had moved out of their shared home in Cambridge Street to Oliver's Court in Westoe. By the time of the 1891 census, they had moved again to Thrift Street, just off South Shields Market Place. Despite being known locally as The King's Highway, Thrift Street could hardly be associated with royalty being, as it was, a central part of the old South Shields, lined with sprawling and dilapidated houses. It suggested times were hard for Peter and Mary Jane. Their youngest son, Thomas Meeks (1875–1934), became Jimmy's grandfather. Thomas Meeks met and married Newcastle born Georgina Jeffels Miller (1884–1939) at the turn of the century and moved into Alderson Street, just off Mile End Road, a stone's throw from South Shields Railway Station. Jimmy's father, John Watson Meeks, their first child, was born in 1901.

Jimmy's mother, Margaret Grieve Christie, was of Scottish descent. Her grandfather John Christie (1832–1883) was born in Dumfries, in the south west of Scotland, and her grandmother, Margaret Grieve (1835–1891), in the border town of Hawick. Margaret's grandparents moved to Liverpool in the 1850s where her father, John Christie, was born in 1855. The family did not stay there long and moved to Maxwell Street in South Shields in the 1860s. Following in his father's footsteps as a slater, the young John Christie set up business as a roofing and slating merchant on Commercial Road. It soon became the daily workplace for most of the male members of the Christie family. In 1883, he married a local girl called Jane Richardson Young (1865–1928). John Christie's business began to prosper and the young Margaret and her siblings soon found themselves living in a brand new terraced house in Landsdowne Terrace in Westoe. However, their good fortune did not last as John Christie began to drink heavily. His neglected empire went into decline and, by 1911, Margaret's family had moved into a two-bedroom flat in Wallis Street, close to the town centre. Two years later John Christie was dead, his business sold off and the money mysteriously missing. His widow and her young family found themselves plunging into a brand of poverty they had never known before. As part of their enforced economy drive, Margaret's mother would often send her running the short distance from their home in Wallis Street to South Shields Market, late on Saturday afternoon, in the hope of picking up a cheap cut of meat for dinner. Tripe, cooked in milk, became one of Margaret's firm favourites!

The Christies did not have any seafaring tradition but were certainly not lacking in moral fibre, many volunteered for military service in the First and Second World Wars. Some did not return.

Jimmy was joined by two brothers, Edward (Teddy) born in 1929, and John born in 1936. John Watson Meeks and his family left their tiny two-roomed flat in Wellington Street, at the top end of Mile End Road in 1937 and moved to the relative spaciousness of 85, Centenary Avenue in the outskirts of town. The timing of the move was ideal for Jimmy since he had just started school at the recently built South Shields High School for Boys which was just around the corner, in Lisle Road. The school had replaced the old Boys' High School in Mowbray Road. The news that Jimmy had even taken the entrance exam came as a complete surprise to his parents. His mother, Margaret, only found out when one of Jimmy's pals stopped her in the street one day and congratulated her on her son's achievement.

As unexpected as Jimmy's exam success was, John Watson Meeks had been determined that his son should not miss out and stumped up the daily bus fare from Wellington Street until they moved to Centenary Avenue. Twenty years earlier, John Watson Meeks had passed the same High School exam but *his* parents could not afford to send him there. The move to Centenary Avenue also opened the door for John and Teddy. John would later attend the same school, but Teddy's early years were blighted by tuberculosis of the spine and his education suffered as a result. He attended Cleadon Park Open School which specialized in the education of children with Tuberculosis and a variety of other illnesses.

Jimmy left South Shields High School for Boys in July 1942 and joined R. Chapman & Son of Newcastle as an apprentice. His motives for joining the Merchant Navy are unclear but it is likely he wanted to follow in the footsteps of several of his uncles who were already Merchant Seamen.

On his first British Seaman's Identity Card, the raven-haired Jimmy Meeks can be seen wearing his small silver-coloured Merchant Navy badge. Not all merchant seamen bothered to wear them, a strong hint that he was quite proud of his new profession. A profession for which he was technically too young since the minimum age for recruits was sixteen. Even that age was considered too young by many and efforts were being made at the time to raise the age limit to seventeen. Not surprisingly, the photograph portrays a picture of innocence but, according to his best friend, Bill Laybourne,

Jimmy was already a typical Meeks, uncompromising and absolutely never afraid to speak his mind. Bill recalled: 'During a dispute with a High School teacher Jimmy threatened to fetch his Dad to sort the teacher out. He went home and promptly returned with him.'

Jimmy's father was frequently involved in street fights. It was in one of these skirmishes that he lost his two front teeth. John Watson Meeks and his brothers worked in the docks together for a company called Wailes and Dove Limited, spraying ships' hulls with bitumen based protective coatings. It was a tough job for tough men. John Watson Meeks died in 1961 as a result of heart and lung failure. He was only 59-years old. Not surprisingly, Jimmy had no intention of following in his father's footsteps.

Jimmy Meeks' Merchant Navy identity card also revealed that he was only 5' 3" at the time of his enrolment. Ordinary Seaman Jack Baron from Hull remembered the young Jimmy Meeks:

'Jimmy and I were good friends. He was a cocky young lad even though he was quite small, but he certainly wasn't a nasty type.'

* * * *

Edward 'Teddy' Briggs Hyde (inset) also had his eye on a career in the Merchant Navy. Born in the town of Cullercoats on the 5th April 1927, the third child of Barbara (née Adamson) and Victor Hyde, he was almost six months younger than his future shipmate Jimmy Meeks. Teddy's brother William 'Billy' was born on the 4th October 1923 and sister, Mary, on the 25th January 1925. A younger sister, Isabel, arrived on the 16th June 1929. Teddy's father, Victor, died in February 1931 aged only 33, leaving his mother with the sole responsibility for bringing up their four children. Fortunately for Barbara, living in the small, closely knit, village community of Cullercoats they had lots of family around them; grandparents, aunts, uncles and cousins, and coped fairly well. Teddy went to Cullercoats Infants' and Boys' School from the time he was 5 until he was 14 years of age.

> *Isabel McGregor (Teddy's sister):* We had a very happy childhood growing up in a secure and loving home, and in a village where everyone knew everyone else. Both boys had paper rounds and all four children helped out at home. Teddy had a carefree childhood, playing on the beaches, cliffs and rock pools with his family and friends.

When war broke out and the bombing started, the Hyde family were separated for the first time when Isabel was evacuated to Hexham with her school, Tynemouth High School. Teddy left Cullercoats Infants' and Boys' School and went to work on a farm in Northallerton, Yorkshire with his cousin Hedley Adamson. Mary had to leave her job and work in an ammunitions factory and Billy joined the RAF. Their mother became an Air Raid Warden for the village and reported to HQ at the Boys' School whenever there was an air raid, and worked with her mother selling fish in South Shields.

Teddy was a natural on the farm working with the animals, but was keen to emulate his older brother's success. Frustratingly, for him, he was too young to join any of the military services. Undaunted, he turned his attention to the Merchant Navy which was not so rigid when it came to the question of age. On the recommendation of an uncle from South Shields, who was already serving in the Merchant Navy, Teddy applied to the shipping company R. Chapman & Son of Newcastle and was rewarded with an apprenticeship in the summer of 1942. He had enjoyed his time on the Northallerton farm but, like Jimmy Meeks, was ready to see the world.

The boys did not have to look hard to find the Merchant Navy. By 1942, it had already been recruiting aggressively for several years. The Merchant Navy Reserve had been founded in 1938 with the mission of finding experienced volunteers willing to serve at sea in the event of an emergency. By the time that emergency arrived in the shape of the Second World War, 13,000 volunteers had already signed up. They would be needed because once war broke out almost 12,000 merchant seamen, many of them Royal Navy Reservists, would immediately transfer to the Royal Navy. The lure of adventure on the high seas saw a steady stream of school leavers volunteering for duty. The Shipping

Federation received hundreds of letters a day from boys asking for work. Forgoing a career in the shipyard with his father, fifteen-year-old Jimmy Meeks, and the six month younger, Teddy Hyde, were two of those eager young men seeking excitement in the Merchant Navy.

Although they would get more excitement than they bargained for, Jimmy Meeks and Teddy Hyde were well aware of the dangers of war for the German Luftwaffe had been dropping bombs on Tyneside for the preceding two years. Most attacks were aimed at the region's shipyards but the first bombs landed, ironically, almost on Jimmy Meeks' doorstep, in a field at the junction of Centenary Avenue and Marsden Road in South Shields on Friday the 21st June 1940. Several houses were damaged by shrapnel but, thankfully, there were no casualties. Later, in October 1941, an unexploded bomb landed in Centenary Avenue. It was successfully dealt with by the Bomb Disposal Squad, which was just as well, since its calibre was between 1,000 and 1,800 kg and would have caused considerable damage had it exploded.

If Jimmy and Teddy were oblivious to the dangers they were about to expose themselves to by joining the Merchant Navy, then a quick look at their new employer's catalogue of shipping losses would have left them in no doubt about the threat posed by the German Navy (Kriegsmarine) in the shape of surface raiders, like *Scharnhorst*, and in particular, the U-boat fleet. R. Chapman & Son had endured a disastrous start to the war, losing ten of their ships and three of the eight Ministry of Transport Ships they were managing. This represented over half of their fleet.

Chapman's was formed in Newcastle in 1878 by sailing ship owners, Ralph Chapman and Thomas R. Miller from

Newcastle, but did not adopt the name R. Chapman & Son until 1896. The company did not actually own any vessels. In order to limit their personal liability, the Chapman family had established two ship owning companies for that purpose: Carlton Steam Ship Company Ltd (1891) and Cambay Steam Ship Company Ltd (1892). The Chapman family retained a 64% controlling stake in all three companies, so for reasons of clarity, these three companies will be referred to as 'Chapman' from now on.

German U-boats were responsible for most of Chapman's losses, accounting for eight of their ships. *SS Tiberton* was the first to go on the 14th February 1940. It had the dubious honour of being sunk by the legendary Otto Kretschmer in U-23, the German Kriegsmarine's most successful U-boat commander, his forty-seven victims amounting to over a quarter of a million tonnes of Allied shipping. The *Tiberton* had been sailing independently from Norway to Middlesbrough with a cargo of iron ore and was torpedoed east of the Orkney Islands in position 58.55N 01.53W. Captain Hugh Mason and the entire crew of thirty-two were lost.

SS Riverton was next to go, caught in Narvik harbour during the German invasion of Norway on the 9th April 1940. One of twenty-seven ships sunk in Narvik between April and June 1940 following heavy fighting in the area; it was actually sunk by a British destroyer during an attempt to recapture Narvik. The crew survived the attack but were force-marched to Sweden by their German captors. Captain J. Nicholson later made a successful escape to Kirkwall with two other Chapman men.

SS Clearton was sunk by U-102 in the Atlantic on the 1st July 1940, 180 miles west of Ushant in position 47.53N

09.30W, while on a voyage from Rosario, Argentina, to Manchester via Freetown with a cargo of 7,320 tons of cereals, a straggler from convoy SL36 comprising forty-one ships. Destroyer *HMS Vansittart* rescued the master, Captain John Edward Elsdon, twenty-four crewmembers and one gunner. Eight of the ship's crew was lost when U-102's second torpedo struck one of the lifeboats as it was being lowered into the water. The survivors would have the satisfaction of seeing U-102 sunk later that day following a successful attack by *HMS Vansittart*, before they were landed in Plymouth.

SS Marbiton was torpedoed and sunk by U-32 in the Atlantic south west of Rockall on the 25th September 1940, in position 56.12N 23.00W while on a voyage from the Tyne to Father Point, New Brunswick, in ballast. It began its voyage in convoy OB216 but had dispersed when attacked by U-32. Captain Reginald Patrick, twenty-three of its crew and one gunner were rescued by *HMS Jason* and *HMS Rochester* and landed at Londonderry. Twelve of its crew died when one of the rescuing destroyers ran over two lifeboats.

SS Carlton was torpedoed by Italian submarine, *Pietro Calvi*, on the 20th December 1940 in the Atlantic north west of Rockall in position 58.30N 18.30W. It had been on a voyage from Newport Mon, Wales, to Buenos Aires in convoy OB260 and carried a cargo of 6,545 tons of coal. It was dispersed from the convoy when attacked. Two lifeboats were launched but one subsequently disappeared. Of the sixteen men in the second lifeboat, only four were alive when they were picked up by the British ship the Antiope on the 7th January 1941. They had been adrift for 18 days in the depth of winter, with sea temperatures around 10°C. The men were in a shocking state, suffering from severe frostbite. Two of the men subsequently had both feet amputated. Captain William Learmount, twenty-nine crewmembers and one gunner died. The *Carlton* survivors' ordeal also made page two of the Times on the 22nd January 1941.

On the 26th September 1940, the master and mate of *SS Demeterton* (2), Chapman's second ship with that name, had a miraculous escape when a 100lb bomb, dropped during a raid on Liverpool Docks, went through the cabin where both men were sitting separately before exploding in the hold below. The bomb missed the Captain's wife by two feet. Upon examination the following day it was discovered that parts of the Mate's wife's hat that had been resting on her bunk were stuck to the nose cone of the bomb. However, their luck ran out six months later when *Demeterton* (2) was sunk on the 16th March 1941 by the German battleship *Scharnhorst*. The Master and crew of *Demeterton* were picked up by *Scharnhorst* and treated to a haircut and a shave by the ship's barber as a token of friendship.

SS Koranton had loaded a general cargo in Philadelphia for Hull and sailed to Sydney, Canada, and joined up with the Liverpool bound 32 ship convoy SC25 that left Sydney on the 10th March 1941. Sometime during the crossing, the *Koranton* fell behind the main convoy and was classed as a straggler when it was torpedoed by U-98 on the 27th March 1941 south west of Reykjavik, Iceland at 59.00N 29.00W. Captain Charles Edward Howard and all thirty-seven crew were lost.

SS Brighton was lost to enemy mines off Dunkirk on the 6th June 1941 whilst carrying a cargo of coal.

SS Empire Dew was the first Ministry of War Transport ship under the management of R. Chapman & Son to be lost. Torpedoed and sunk by U-48 on the 12th June 1941. It had been sailing independently in ballast from Tyne to Father Point, New Brunswick, dispersed from convoy OG64, when attacked and sunk at position 51.09N 30.16W. RN Destroyer, *HMS St Albans*, rescued Captain John Edward Elsdon, sixteen crew and 2 gunners. Twenty-three of its crew were lost.

SS Frumenton, the largest vessel in the Chapman fleet, was lost in very unfortunate circumstances on the 4th March 1942 when a German aircraft dropped a parachute mine directly in front of it almost within sight of its London destination. The resulting explosion under the engine room broke its back. An attempt was made to tow the crippled ship home by two tugboats but it sank off Orffordness.

SS Empire Cowper, another Ministry ship, was sunk on the 11th April 1942 by enemy aircraft while returning home from a voyage to Russia. *SS Fort Good Hope* was sunk by U-159 (Witte) in the Atlantic on the 11th June 1942, north west of Colon, Panama, in position 10.00N 80.16W while sailing independently on a voyage from Vancouver to Garston. Captain Horatio Gentiles, forty crew and four gunners were rescued by the US gunboat *Erie* and landed at Cristobel.

The *Earlston*, one of the ten ships built for Chapman's by Burntisland Shipbuilding in Glasgow during the war years, was sunk by U-334 on the 5th July 1942 at position 74.45N 37.40E on a voyage from Glasgow to Archangel. It was part of the ill-fated convoy PQ17. Chased and bombed by dive-bombers, the convoy had already dispersed when a near miss exploded near to the *Earlston*'s engine room stopping it dead. By the time U-334 torpedoed and sank the crippled ship, it had already been abandoned. One lifeboat made it to Russia from where the occupants were repatriated, while the second lifeboat reached Norway only to be captured and made prisoners of war. Captain H. J. Stenwick was taken as prisoner onboard U-334. He received a Distinguished Service Cross for his actions during the attack. Eleven other crewmembers received decorations for bravery, including Apprentice Andrew Watt who was awarded the British Empire Medal and the Lloyd's Medal for Bravery at Sea.

Despite these heavy losses, R. Chapman & Son's directors Mr. R. Chapman and Mr. C. I. Willan decided to lobby the Ministry with a proposal to replace their losses by ordering ships directly to their account rather than joining the queue for ships to be issued by the Ministry of War Transport. Their unusual proposal was accepted with the provision that the company use a standard design and that Short Bros. receive their orders. However, Short Bros were fully occupied, so Burntisland Shipbuilding Ltd of Glasgow picked up the orders instead. They built ten ships for Chapman's and only one of them failed to survive the war (*SS Earlston*). This risky, but ultimately successful, policy of wartime replacement raised the number of vessels in the Chapman fleet to fifteen by the end of the war, ironically the same number they had at the start of the War. Only four of the original fifteen were still afloat at the end of hostilities. The four originals were newer ships and together with the modern vessels built during the war years, R. Chapman & Son could boast a modern and comparatively large fleet that was able to take advantage of the cargo boom at the end of the War, while other shipping companies found themselves scrambling to replace their fleet (some had lost all their vessels). This predictably resulted in higher prices at the shipyards, which was in Chapman's favour since their competitors' ships cost more.

Although the remnants of Chapman's fleet in 1942 were

made up of mostly modern vessels, Jimmy Meeks and Teddy Hyde found themselves allocated to one of Chapman's oldest ships, *SS Peterton*. Only *SS Innerton* was older and it was on its last legs, destined to be donated to the Ministry of War Transport for the Normandy landings and used as a blocking ship in a Mulberry Harbour (temporary harbour used to offload cargo on beaches).

Built in 1919 by Richardson, Duck and Co. Ltd, *SS Peterton* (5,221 GRT, 400.1 x 52.4 x 28.4 feet) was a vessel that probably would have been heading for a similar fate to the Innerton and no doubt offered just as little in the way of comfort, especially having been damaged twice during bombing raids; but the necessities of war and Chapman's dwindling fleet meant that it would have to soldier on.

R. Chapman & Son built four vessels in 1919. Three of them; *SS Peterton*, *SS Innerton* and *SS Clearton* failed to see out the war but by then had made invaluable contributions to the company. The fourth vessel built that year, *SS Linnerton*, suffered a disastrously short career. Its engines broke down on its maiden voyage to Baltimore in December 1919, and when the crippled vessel was towed back to the Tyne, it broke anchor in bad weather and ended up stranded on South Shields Beach, where it broke in two and was declared a constructive total loss. Barely a month had passed since its launch. It would remain there until May 1920 when the bow and stern sections were refloated and towed to Rotterdam where they were ingeniously reassembled and modified to make a tanker for the Anglo Saxon Petroleum Company. The *Linnerton* was sold and renamed several times before being impounded by the Mexican government in 1940 and finally foundering on a voyage to New York in 1944.

R. Chapman & Son of Newcastle, WW2 Fleet:

SHIP	GRT	BUILT	FATE	LOST
Innerton	5297	1919	▼ Scuttled in Mulberry Harbour	09.06.1944
Clearton	5219	1919	▼ Sunk by U-102	01.07.1940
Mabriton	6694	1920	▼ Sunk by U-32	25.09.1940
Tiberton	5225	1920	▼ Sunk by U-23	14.02.1940
Koranton	6695	1920	▼ Sunk by U-98	27.03.1941
Carlton (4)	5162	1924	▼ Sunk by CALVI (Italy) – U-boat	27.12.1940
Demerterton (2)	5251	1928	▼ Sunk by Battleship Scharnhorst	16.01.1941
Brighton (2)	5359	1928	▼ Sunk by mines off Dunkirk	06.05.1941
Riverton (2)	5378	1928	▼ Sunk by British Destroyer, Narvik	20.04.1940
Amberton	5377	1928	Stranded Western Head, Cape Pine	1947
Grainton	6341	1929	Sold 1950. Broken up in Yokosuka	1960
Nurtureton	6272	1929	Sold 1953. Broken up in Hong Kong	1960
Frumenton (1)	6675	1930	▼ Sunk by mines off Orfordness	04.03.1942
Generton	4801	1936	Sold 1955. Broken up in Kaohsiung	1969
Hermiston	4795	1939	Sold 1960. Wrecked – Naoetsu	1967
Scorton	4795	1939	Sold 1955. Sank on voyage to Da Nang	1967
Merton	5095	1941	Sold 1960. Wrecked on voyage to Japan	1964
Norton	5081	1941	Sold 1956. Chinese Government.	>1985
Earlston	7195	1941	▼ Sunk by U-334	05.07.1942
Allerton	5079	1941	Sold 1957. Broken up in Kaohsiung	1968
Ingleton	5023	1942	Sold 1960. Broken up in Sakai	1967
Carlton (5)	5035	1942	Sold 1963. Broken up in Hong Kong	1964
Brighton (3)	7345	1943	Sold 1959. Broken up in Hong Kong	1965
Riverton (3)	7345	1943	Sold 1960. Broken up in Kaohsiung	1969
Demeterton (3)	7344	1944	Sold 1963. Broken up in Kaohsiung	1971
Frumenton (2)	7542	1919	Sold 1962. Broken up in Hong Kong	1970
Empire Dew	7005	1941	▼ Sunk by U-48	12.06.1941
Empire Liberty	7157	1941	Returned 1945. Broken up in Osaka	1960
Empire Cowper	7164	1941	▼ Bombed and sunk by aircraft	11.04.1942
Fort Good Hope	7130	1942	▼ Sunk by U-159	11.06.1942

▼ *Vessels sunk during World War Two*

SS *Peterton*'s record in the war up to 1942 was impressive. It had carried a great variety of essential cargos across the Atlantic, repeatedly running the gauntlet of the U-boat wolf packs. Its first brush with the enemy came on the 26th September 1940 in Brunswick Dock, Liverpool, when it was bombed and damaged in an air raid. A few months later, on the 24th December 1940, it received an early Christmas present when attacked by German aircraft and was left damaged by bombs. It had sailed in large convoys, such as HX130 that departed Halifax, Nova Scotia, on the 1st June 1941 bound for Liverpool (convoy pendant 13), where its cargo of wheat and trucks arrived safely and uneventfully in Liverpool on the 20th June 1941. But as part of convoy SC42, the *Peterton* would find itself in the midst of one of the epic U-boat battles of the Second World War. Convoy SC42 departed Sydney, Canada, on the 30th August 1941 and arrived in Liverpool on the 15th September 1941. Of the sixty five ships that left Sydney, sixteen were sunk and one damaged. The *Peterton* (convoy pendant 82) and its cargo of sugar were amongst the battered survivors. It sailed in the second row of ships behind the *Gypsum Queen*, which was one of the vessels sunk.

SS *Peterton* had been a lucky ship and had been protected by some brave men: Gunner Robert Sydney Charles Turner received a Commendation which was reported in the Merchant Navy Awards section of the London Gazette on the 10th June 1941 for his actions onboard the ship.

3

HUNTER AND HUNTED

Jimmy Meeks and Teddy Hyde were still at school when Commander Heinrich Bleichrodt and his U-boat, U-109, disembarked from Lorient on the west coast of France on the 18th July 1942, on a patrol that would see their paths cross in dramatic fashion. Commander Heinrich 'Ajax' Bleichrodt was U-109's second and, as it turned out, most successful commander. He had begun his U-boat career in October 1939 and served his time on the cadet ship Gorch Fock and the heavy cruiser Admiral Hipper, before he took command of a small training boat, U-8. From June to July 1940, he completed one patrol as First Watch Officer (IWO) with U-34 under Commander Wilhelm Rollmann. They sank eight ships totalling 22,434 tons.

In August 1940, he assumed command of U-48, and on the 8th September 1940, began his first patrol as a commander. Onboard, as his IWO, was Teddy Suhren. Together they sank eight ships totalling 36,189 tons. Their second patrol in October 1940 was also a great success with eight ships sunk totalling 43,106 tons. Three days before their return from that patrol, U-48 received a radio transmission regarding a Knights Cross that had been awarded. When Bleichrodt learned that it was for him, he refused to wear his new medal until his IWO, Teddy Suhren received one as well, since he had overseen all surface shooting on previous missions. On the 3rd November 1940, Suhren became the first IWO to receive the Knights Cross for his "outstanding part in the sinking of more then 200,000 tons".

In autumn 1940, Bleichrodt left U-48 and in January 1941 commissioned U-67. Then, on the 5th June 1941, he assumed command of U-109. U-109 had been laid down on the 9th March 1940 at AG Weser in Bremen and commissioned later that year on the 5th December 1940. U-109 was allocated to the 2nd U-boat Flottille and, under the guidance of its first commander, Hans-Georg Fischer, its crew underwent training from the 5th December 1940 to the 30th April 1941. Its maiden combat voyage, which began on the 1st May 1941, almost ended in disaster when the boat came within a whisker of sinking. U-109 had been tracking a convoy (HX126) heading east out of Newfoundland when it had been attacked by six British destroyers. During a sixteen-hour stand-off, a faulty pressure gauge had seen them plummet unintentionally to a depth of 600 feet. No U-boat had ever been that deep before and seen the light of day again. In a desperate attempt to raise the boat, the Chief Engineer had clumsily put it at an angle of 60° causing the stern to fill with bilge water and push U-109 even deeper to a hull crushing 900 feet. The Chief Engineer thought nothing more could be done and resigned himself to death. In a last ditch effort to save the boat, Petty Officer Otto Peters had taken control of the blow valve panel. He quickly realised that Chief Engineer Weber had only blown the stern tanks in his attempt to raise the boat. Weber had ignored the leaking forward tanks assuming they were useless. By transferring air from the stern tanks to the forward tanks, which were 150 feet higher due to the angle of the boat, he was able to get the boat to rise despite the leaks. As the bow began to rise, the air in the forward tanks started to expand and soon the boat was accelerating to the surface, to the great relief of Hirschfeld and the rest of the crew. Their relief was soon tempered by the realisation that the destroyers would be waiting for them. On the surface, Commander Fischer gave the order to abandon ship. Many of the crew were already on the U-boat deck when someone noticed that the destroyers had gone. U-109 limped back to Lorient in May 1941, where Fischer was subsequently dismissed from the U-boat Arm and Otto Peters was awarded an Iron Cross. Chief Engineer Weber's shortcomings were the main reason for U-109's problems but Fischer's unpopularity amongst his officers meant that he would be made ultimately responsible. Weber himself continued to serve on U-109 but, after further mishaps under Bleichrodt, was transferred to U-526.

U-109's movements in the summer of 1942 are well documented thanks to the work of Herbert Ritschel who published three volumes of U-boat war diaries (Kriegstagebücher or 'KTB' for short) covering U-1 through U-124. They are not as detailed as the full KTBs but they do generally have the most important information. U-boat commanders were required to maintain a war diary in accordance with Standing War Order of BdU No. 501: *Keeping of War Diaries*:

> 'War diaries of U-boats are to be completed immediately after return from each operation. A new one is then to be started at once, beginning with the lay days in harbour or dock, and carried on continuously until after the next operation. It must afford a continuous review of the activities and positions of the boat.'

KTBs were hand written by the commander during a patrol and if the U-boat returned in once piece, they were typed out. Copies were then sent to the Naval High Command, BdU Operations and Administration and to the Flotilla. The KTB's are available for research today thanks to Admiral Dönitz who ordered the Kriegsmarine archives to be preserved and allowed them to be seized intact by the Allies.

U-109's movements in the summer of 1942 are also documented in the book *Secret Diary of a U-boat* written by its radio operator Wolfgang Hirschfeld. In chapter 8, titled *Oakleaves for The Commander*, he describes U-109's sixth combat mission in graphic detail. The kind of detail given in this account is extremely rare. Only U-boat commanders were permitted to keep a diary during patrols; and they tended to be formal accounts for the KTB, concentrating on ships attacked and fuel situations. Radio operator Wolfgang Hirschfeld's book is spiced with lively dialogue and keen observations and is a first class account of the Battle of The Atlantic from the perspective of a frontline U-boat.

The story began on the 5th July 1942 when Radio Operator Wolfgang Hirschfeld arrived in Lorient, after three weeks of home leave. He joined the crew of U-109 which was commanded once again by Heinrich Bleichrodt. First Lieutenant Joachim Schramm, a former E-boat man, was the new face onboard. Several of the officers were seasoned campaigners but the majority of the crew were young and inexperienced and were likened to a kindergarten by one of the senior officers.

Three days after Hirschfeld arrived in Lorient; the newly overhauled and painted U-109 left the base. It was in good shape and ready for its sixth patrol. The same could not be said of Commander Heinrich Bleichrodt. After three years of war his nerves were beginning to show signs of frailty and the prospect of running the gauntlet of British destroyers and Liberator bombers in the increasingly perilous Bay of Biscay did little to lift his spirits. It did not take long before the first depth charges began to hammer U-109 and its inexperienced crew. Commander Bleichrodt had to steel himself before he gave reassuring glances to the crew. To divert his, and the crew's, thoughts Bleichrodt carried out a series of emergency drills as they crept towards the safety of the open Atlantic.

Meanwhile, *SS Peterton* was over 3,000 miles away in the West African port of Freetown, Sierra Leone. Skippered by Captain Thomas William Marrie (34) from Sunderland, the *Peterton* had been laid up in port in Freetown since the 29th June 1942. Several of its crew were being treated for ailments and illnesses ranging from broken bones, septic sores, sexually transmitted diseases (two cases) and malaria. They had begun their voyage in the Welsh port of Barry on the 17th April and, after stops in Glasgow and Takoradi in Ghana, would soon be leaving Freetown for the long voyage home. It was not a popular place.

> *J. A. Morley:* I stopped in Freetown many times. It was the arsehole of Africa!

BdU contacted U-109 on the 14th July and ordered them to head for the Brazilian coast. On the same day, the *Peterton* left Freetown as part of a 33-ship convoy (SL116) bound for London. They were joined in the convoy by *SS Nyanza*. Onboard were three men who would soon be joining the *Peterton*: Chas Smith (19) from Hull, his pal, Ray Tennant

(24) from Canada and George Pennington (19) from Wigan. The slow moving convoy was expected to take three weeks to reach England, but its size and posse of escorts would make it difficult for any U-boats thinking of launching an attack.

On the 7th August, U-109's bridge watch reported the silhouette of a large passenger ship on a westerly heading travelling at more than 20 knots, a speed they could never hope to match. U-109 began to chase but soon realised it was futile and gave up. Commander Bleichrodt later admitted to Hirschfeld his mixed feelings about attacking passenger ships since they often carried women and children. Bleichrodt had good reason to be sceptical – earlier in the war, as commander of U48; he had sunk an evacuee ship, *City of Benares*, which had been travelling from the United Kingdom to Canada. Bleichrodt was devastated when he later learned he had been responsible for the death of 77 of the 90 children onboard.

Commander Bleichrodt also received word from BdU that there was no longer any fuel available for his boat since the fuel tanker (U-460) scheduled to meet them was empty. Ironically, the crew treated this as great news since they liked the idea of spending the rest of the war in Rio. Later that evening, Bleichrodt's attention turned to more pressing matters when a ship was spotted heading north at a more leisurely 10 knots. The ship was the Norwegian registered tanker *Arthur W. Sewall* (6,035 BRT). Submerged, Bleichrodt observed the steamer through his periscope. He used it sparingly as the sea was unusually calm, making them easier to spot. Armed with a 10.5 cm stern gun and several machine guns, the tanker was more than capable of defending itself on the surface. Bleichrodt waited until he was within 1,000 yards and then fired two torpedoes. Ninety seconds later they smashed into the bow and stern of the tanker. The *Arthur W. Sewall* stopped dead in its tracks and listed heavily to starboard; but it was far from finished! Its master ordered all guns to be manned and then set the ship on an even keel through some prudent ballasting. Bleichrodt ordered a fresh attack but, just as they fired off a third torpedo, the *Arthur W. Sewall* moved off and the torpedo passed safely by. U-109 set off in pursuit. Forty minutes later they were in position again and fired off a fourth torpedo. This time *Arthur W. Sewall* was unable to avoid a direct and fatal hit. Its crew abandoned their guns and prepared to abandon ship. Boatsman, Eduard Maureschat, finished it off with multiple hits from U-109's deck cannon. *Arthur W. Sewall* sank at 08.47N 34.35W. U-109 failed to capture the ship's master since the lifeboats were gone by the time they reached the wreck site. Later, BdU ordered a reluctant Bleichrodt to divert his attention to Freetown, despite his preference (for tactical reasons), and the crew's preference (for social reasons), to operate off Brazil.

SS *Peterton* docked in Gravesend on the 10th August 1942. It had been an uneventful three weeks, though several of the crew had gone down with malaria during the voyage. One crew member, who had been accused of malingering during the entire voyage, left the ship and duly obtained a medical certificate from a local doctor. He did not return.

The following morning, U-109 was patrolling south of Cape Verde when the hydrophone operator reported a sound similar to a propeller through his headphones. Although uncertain that the sound was from a propeller, Bleichrodt, the eternal optimist, set off in the direction of this mysterious sound. His persistence was rewarded when, later that afternoon, they spotted the mastheads of an Allied tanker. U-

109 crash-dived and, with its electric motors at full throttle, Bleichrodt put his boat in a position to launch torpedoes from their stern mounted torpedo tubes. Two direct hits broke the tanker in two and set it ablaze. U-109 waited until the lifeboats were clear of the wreck before surfacing and approaching the lifeboats. The vessel was identified as Glasgow registered *Vimeira* (5,728 BRT). Its master, Captain Norman Ross Caird, was arrested and taken onboard U-109. SS *Vimeira* was lost at 10.05N 28.92W. U-109 continued on its planned course to Freetown with their new prisoner onboard.

Wolfgang Hirschfeld (U-109): **Captain Caird adapted readily to U-boat life, although he admitted to an uncomfortable feeling whenever we dived very deep. He appeared to relish Järschel's cooking, and when he politely declined any more of our German cigarettes, I let him have some of my cigars instead.**

After a brief stop at Ford's plant in Dagenham, the *Peterton* arrived in Hull on the 16th August 1942 and paid off its tired crew.

U-109 reached its designated patrol off Freetown on the 19th August but, as feared by Bleichrodt, there were no ships in the vicinity and, with fuel resources dwindling; they were soon heading north and home to Lorient.

Accompanied by his mother, Barbara, 15-year old Teddy Hyde left the comfort and safety of his home in Cullercoats on the 21st August and travelled by train to Hull where he joined his first ship, *SS Peterton*. His sister, Isabel McGregor, recalled her brother's farewell visit made only days before he was scheduled to start his active Merchant Navy career:

'I was staying with my grandmother in Glanton, Northumberland. Teddy came by bus to say "Cheerio" to us – quite a journey by bus from Cullercoats. Only 15 years old, but I thought he looked quite grown up and very smart in his Merchant Navy uniform. He could easily have passed for 18 years old. He wanted me to come back with him to Cullercoats: "Come on kidda!" he said, in an attempt to persuade me to travel back with him. I couldn't go of course.'

Teddy's mother, tried everything in her power to stop her son from joining the Merchant Navy, but he was, in his sister Isabel's words, 'a very strong personality who made his mark'. Teddy refused to be swayed. On her return to Cullercoats, Barbara Hyde confided chillingly to a relative: 'I will never see that lad again!'

Jimmy Meeks left his home in Centenary Avenue, South Shields and travelled to Hull on the 24th August 1942. When he got there he found the *Peterton* undergoing repairs and in the process of loading 6,000 tons of washed coal in preparation for its next voyage. Teddy Hyde was relieved to be joined by someone his own age. Shipping companies frequently assigned apprentices in pairs to ensure they had someone of similar age to work and socialise with.

Although the two boys had plenty of pluck, they were grossly lacking in experience. This would be provided by men like Able Seaman John 'Jack' Albert Morley (inset), who had just joined the *Peterton* after leaving his last ship, SS Reynolds (5,113 GRT). Although only three years older than Jimmy and Teddy; Jack had plenty of experience. The Reynolds had been his second ship of the war. One of his voyages on the Reynolds had been a real marathon affair, sailing from the United States, heading around Cape Horn and through the Suez Canal to Egypt, carrying a cargo of tanks, landing launches and planes for the North African campaign.

Jack Morley had grown up in Hull, the third of five children by John Ernest and Grace Evelyn Morley, and trained for a career at sea before war broke out, attending Nautical School from the age of 13. His home town had received a pounding in the first three years of the war by the German Luftwaffe, who recognised it as an important industrial centre and port. By the end of the war, 95% of Hull's houses would have received some form of damage, leaving over half of the 320,000 population homeless and 1,200 people dead. Only London would come off worse. The main docks – Albert, Alexandra, St Andrews, King George V and Victoria – all suffered direct hits from a variety of bombs.

Jack Morley had initially set his mind on a career on Hull's trawlers, but when the war stated and they were impounded by the government, he was forced to seek work on merchant ships instead. Jack's father was also a sailor and had worked as a cook on fishing boats for years, despite losing a leg in the trenches of the First World War.

J. A. Morley: It was my first time on the *Peterton*. I didn't know anyone when I mustered on board. I had my 'donkey's breakfast' mattress with me. It was well worn after years of use and looked more like a bundle of oats.

(Left) *Jack Morley (Hull), SS Reynolds, May 1942*. Standing in a motor launch with crewmate, Dick Clark, bound for Alexandria, Egypt. Later that year, Clark would lose his life when the Empire Stevenson was destroyed by enemy aircraft in convoy PQ18, on its way to Russia. *(J. A. Morley – Private)*

Jack was not particularly impressed when he stepped aboard the *Peterton* for the first time.

J. A. Morley: Well, it was a wreck and really showing its age.

Most of the *Peterton*'s previous crew, who had been paid off when they had arrived in Hull on the 17th August 1942, did not return. Only the Master, Captain Thomas Marrie, 1st Engineer Thomas Cuthbert Gorman, 1st Radio Officer Jonathan Davies, Chief Steward Archie Swan, 3rd Mate Ernest Thompson and Merchant Navy Gunner William Lytle signed on for its next voyage. Since the majority of these men were senior officers, they, like U-109, were able to keep the crewmembers central to its day-to-day running.

Many of the replacements who arrived in the days after docking in Hull hailed from the local area. The most senior member of the Hull contingent was 43-year-old veteran 2nd Officer George Denis Howes. He was accompanied by Able Seaman Frank Nock (20), Able Seaman George Norfolk (27) – the ship's unofficial comedian – 4th Engineer Walter March (20) on his first voyage, Sailor George Keay (19), Ordinary Seaman James Henry Stephenson (22), Ordinary Seaman John 'Jack' Albert Morley (18), Firemen: Charles Smith (19), Alan Goodfellow (18), Samuel Osborne (31) and Herbert Weaver, Greaser Albert Richardson (39) and Cabin Boy Dennis Harold Thirkettle (19).

The remaining members of the *Peterton*'s compliment was made up by: 1st Officer Francis Buller Fairweather (42) from East Ham, Reginald Harrison from Scunthorpe, Army Gunners: Albert Lewington (25) from London, and Sydney Ludlam (21) from Sheffield, Royal Navy Gunners: Albert Hickling (35) from Leicester, and Ronald Minney (21) from Caterham, Merchant Navy Gunners William Brooks (18) from Preston, and W. E. Lambie (28) from Bristol, Fireman Hati Chand (24) from Trinidad, Galley Boy Michael Byrne (17) from Goole, Bosun John S. Watt (59) from Lerwick, Sheltand Islands, Sailor George Pennington (19) from Wigan, and Sailor John Ennis (27) from Wexford, Ireland.

SS Peterton, like most merchant vessels of the period, was well armed. It carried one 4" stern gun, one 12 Pounder mounted at the bow, two Twin Marlins, two Lewis guns and four P. A. C. (Parachute and Cable) rockets. These were manned by the *Peterton*'s two Army gunners, two Royal Navy gunners and three Merchant Navy gunners. This combination of gunners from the three different services was quite typical at that time in the war. They were collectively known as DEMS (Defensively Equipped Merchant Ship) gunners. They were the result of an Admiralty Trade Division program established in June, 1939, with the intention of arming British merchant ships. Personnel were mobilised from the Army, Royal Navy and Merchant Navy, men being trained to load and operate the weaponry to make up a shortfall in numbers.

One of the two Army gunners onboard the *Peterton* was twenty-one year old Sydney Ludlam (inset) from Sheffield. Ludlam had just completed his training at 5th Maritime Artillery in Shoeburyness and was on his first voyage. He was partnered by Albert Lewington who, as the more experienced man, was assigned to look after him.

Merchant Navy Gunner William Brooks was also on his first ship, meaning that, together with Walter March, Sydney Ludlam and the two apprentices, five members of the crew were on their maiden voyage.

Jimmy Meeks and Teddy Hyde were stationed mid-ships, together with the officers. The deck and engine-room crew were stationed in cabins aft of the ship. According to Jack Morley, the officers and apprentices were not encouraged to socialise with the crew. This was a source of aggravation to Jack who felt many officers relied on people like him for training and experience.

Jimmy and Teddy did not have to wait long to get their first taste of life at sea. There was a war to win, merchant seamen were in short supply and the pressure was on to keep them as active as possible. Even in war, merchant ships continued to criss-cross the globe carrying cash cargoes as well as vital war supplies.

Shortly after Jimmy Meeks boarded the ship, and with their cargo loading completed, Captain Thomas Marrie ordered their departure from Hull Dock. The plan was to proceed to Oban on the North West coast of Scotland and join convoy OS39, scheduled to sail for Freetown, leaving Oban on the 30th August 1942 and picking up more ships from Liverpool on the way. Once off Freetown, the convoy would disperse and the *Peterton* could proceed alone to its final destination of Buenos Aires, Argentina.

U-109 meanwhile was lurking south-west of Liberia off the coast of West Africa and Commander Bleichrodt was frustrated by the lack of action. Despite this, and an open invitation from BdU to operate further south, Bleichrodt demurred since he knew their dwindling fuel resources prevented this. Only 68 cubic metres of their 208 cubic metre capacity remained, leaving the boat with a range of around 3,000 nautical miles, roughly its distance from their base in Lorient, France. In an attempt to galvanise BdU, he contacted them and announced his intention to head for home. It had the desired effect for Dönitz himself intervened and promised 38 cubic metres and ordered Bleichrodt to remain in position.

Following its departure from Hull on the 24th August, records maintained at the National Archives reveal that the *Peterton* did not in fact sail directly to Oban but instead docked two days later in the port of Methil on the east coast of Scotland. *SS Peterton* left Methil on the 28th August but no longer harboured any realistic hope of reaching Oban in time to rendezvous with convoy OS39. Failure to sail with OS39 would have dramatic consequences for the ship and its crew for convoy OS39 would arrive safely in Freetown whilst the *Peterton* was now on a collision course with U-109.

Captain Thomas Marrie was an experienced campaigner and would not have delayed his departure from Methil without very good reason. So why did he keep the *Peterton* docked in Methil for four valuable days? It was not unusual for ships to pull out of convoys for a multitude of reasons: engine problems and shortages of crew being two of the more common causes. There was no evidence that the *Peterton* was suffering from mechanical problems, however, they did lack one essential crewmember, their cook! The man assigned to the job, John M. Taylor (24) from Grimsby, had, in the words of the ship's indignant master, 'deserted' on the 21st August. Taylor had visited the Shipping Registrar's Panel doctor on the 24th August and had been diagnosed with Colitis but certified fit enough for duty, provided his treatment was continued at sea. Since Taylor did not have enough time to get to his own doctor to start treatment before the *Peterton* left port he decided not to sail. Later, his own doctor confirmed the diagnosis, but went further than the Registrar's panel doctor by certifying Taylor as unfit for duty. Taylor's illness was clearly genuine since the Registrar's own solicitors advised against any disciplinary action. A six-week voyage to Buenos Aires without a regular cook was an unthinkable proposition for Marrie, leaving him no other option than to put into port and pick up a replacement. Geo Fisher (34) from Sunderland was the man chosen for the job and made the journey north to Methil, joining up with the *Peterton* on the 28th August 1942. Fisher was a seasoned campaigner and had come directly from *Peterton*'s sister ship, *SS Ingleton*. An extra fireman, William Haughton, who lived in Methil, also joined the vessel there. The *Peterton*'s crew now numbered forty-three.

Whenever a ship failed to meet a convoy, it was normal procedure for it to simply wait for the next one; and since OS convoys sailed with great regularity; the crew of the *Peterton* should not have long to wait. However, instead of delaying until the 9th September for the next planned OS convoy to Freetown, Captain Thomas Marrie received orders from his employer to continue to Oban and join convoy OG89 which was scheduled to leave Liverpool on the 1st September 1942. This was clearly a compromise since the *Peterton*'s destination was still Buenos Aires and convoy OG89, which was a Gibraltar convoy, could only take them as far as the Azores. From there they would have to sail alone and unescorted for several days inside U-boat territory.

The Freetown bound convoy OS39 left Liverpool on the 31st August and sailed into the Irish Sea and up the west coast of Scotland and out into the North Atlantic without the *Peterton*.

The *Peterton* arrived belatedly in Oban on 1st September and took its allotted station in convoy OG89. They sailed to Liverpool, where more ships joined the convoy, bringing its total to 21. The *Peterton* was clearly the odd man out in this convoy, being the only ship with a destination in the South Atlantic.

Three thousand miles away, U-109 was still patrolling the African coast south of Freetown. Its ever watchful lookouts had spotted the mastheads of a large steamer. *SS Ocean Might* (7,173 BRT) was alone but moving rapidly at 14 knots and skippered by the highly experienced Captain William James Park. It was late in the evening and the U-boat men lost sight

List of Ships – Convoy OG89:

NAME/STATION NR.	CARGO	DESTINATION
Accrington 053	Rescue Ship	1st Voyage
Almenara 081	Coke	Cadiz
Baron Forbes 052	Coal	Lisbon
CARA 071	Coke	Huelva
Empire Cabot 072	General	Gibraltar
Empire Caxton 041	Coal	Lisbon
Empire Franklin 082	Stores, Coal Cam	Gibraltar
Empire Gazelle 051	Stores	Gibraltar
Empire Heath 012	Coal Cam	Gibraltar
Empire Kestrel 021	General	Lisbon
Empire Tern 061	General	Seville
Finland 032	Red Cross Stores	Lisbon
Grodno 062	Stores, Cement	Gibraltar
Merkland 023 Br 1	General	Lisbon
Ogmore Castle 042	Coal	Lisbon
Ottinge 033	Coal	Lisbon
Ousel 031	Coal	Lisbon
Pacific 022	Coal	Returned
Peterton 073	Coal	**Buenos Aires**
Phillip M 063	Coke	Straggled
Shetland 011	POW Mail, Coal	Lisbon Straggled

of the ship against a dark bank of cloud. This forced Bleichrodt to guess the ship's possible course in the hope of intercepting her the following morning.

Their calculations were spot on as the *Ocean Might* appeared off their starboard bow early the next day. The ship was steering a zigzag course, making it very difficult for U-109 to get into a firing position. After almost a day of trying, U-109 finally launched three torpedoes but all missed their target as the *Ocean Might* cannily changed its course for the umpteenth time. Another shot fired shortly afterwards also failed to hit its target. Captain Park's tactics were not only beneficial to his own ship's chances of survival but also contributed greatly to the safety of other ships as Bleichrodt wasted one deadly torpedo after another. U-109 continued its pursuit and by the evening fired a fifth torpedo, which turned out to be a dud. A sixth torpedo eventually slammed into the *Ocean Might*'s stern. Once its lifeboats were clear of the sinking ship, a seventh torpedo was fired to finish the job. It had been an expensive attack in terms of munitions. It was late and the falling darkness allowed the lifeboats to disappear before Bleichrodt had a chance to question any of the survivors. He expressed his regret at not being able to meet the master, who, he reckoned, was 'a really experienced type'. They set a course south and were soon crossing the equator and into the South Atlantic.

The destination of the *Peterton*'s voyage was withheld from the crew until the ship was well out to sea. This measure was intended to reduce the risk of convoy details falling into enemy hands.

The apprentices were thrilled to learn that their maiden voyage would take them to Buenos Aires in Argentina. The more experienced crew members were also happy with the destination since it promised weeks of stress-free sailing in the warm and relatively U-boat free South Atlantic. As long as they made it safely to Freetown on the return leg, they could expect to hook up with a northbound convoy as they had done back in July.

Jack Morley: We had been at sea several days before we learned our destination was Buenos Aires; and that only came via the rumour mill.

The boys' first few weeks at sea were a baptism of fire. It is comforting to imagine they were given light duties but the reality was probably quite different.

Jack Baron: They were often given jobs that the experienced men were not permitted to do by the unions.

These were sentiments shared by other seamen who noted that apprentices were often treated better by the crew than their senior officers. As a result, they often preferred to socialise with the crew during shore leave. Fraternising with the crew onboard was not encouraged, even though the apprentices were taught many of their practical skills by them.

In the early hours of the 3rd September, 2nd Officer George Howes' previous ship, *SS Hollinside*, was sunk by the notorious German U-boat, U-107. It had been travelling in small unescorted convoy on its way to Almeira from the port of Lisbon when hit by one of two torpedoes fired by U-107. Three of its crew were killed and the survivors picked up and landed back in Lisbon.

U-109 was patrolling the Freetown to Cape Town route and had been doing so for several days but, after no further sightings, they turned north-east on the 6th September and headed back towards the Gulf of Guinea. Later the same evening, they spotted the masts of a large steamer to the east; it was heading straight across their bow. Two torpedoes were fired at a range of 800 yards, both of which slammed into the hull of the steamer. It stopped immediately and the lifeboats were launched. The victim was the refrigerator ship *SS Tuscan Star* (11,449 BRT) sunk at 0.57N 11.67W. It had been carrying 7,840 tons of frozen meat and 5,000 tons of general stores from Buenos Aires and had been bound for London. In accordance with BdU procedure, Bleichrodt ordered his crew to approach the lifeboats in order to capture the ship's master, but on seeing there were women and children in the lifeboats, he summoned one of his officers to gather some provisions for them. This was a relatively generous gesture since they too were low on supplies, although they could expect to replenish their own stocks at the next refuelling rendezvous, which should not be long considering their fuel situation. As the provisions were being gathered, the U-boat men crew heard a cry for help and directed their searchlight towards a desperate voice coming from the water. They spotted a man struggling amongst the wreckage. Eduard Maureschat, the Boatsman who had skilfully finished off the *Arthur W. Sewall* with his deck cannon, dived into the sea and saved the drowning man. The fortunate survivor was one of the *Tuscan Star*'s radio operators, Gordon Gill. The lifeboats were packed with survivors, some of them half-naked, but none the less, fifty two of the 113 persons onboard had been killed in the attack. The lifeboats moved alongside U-109 and, after taking onboard two sacks of supplies, a polite exchange of thanks and good-luck was made and then the lifeboats drifted away.

    The crew of U-109 were not unusual in making this rapid transition from heartless purveyors of atrocity to Good Samaritans, prepared to risk their lives to save a drowning individual or donate provisions they badly needed themselves.

Commander Bleichrodt was very conscious of the image he and his crew portrayed to their victims and reported their encounter with the *Arthur W. Sewall*'s survivors in his diary:

Heinrich Bleichrodt (U-109) – KTB U-boat Diary:
06.09.1942
Commander: Hopefully, these people are now cured of their belief that all Germans are barbarians.

Only the faceless and indiscriminate nature of the U-boat war made it possible to behave in this manner. Once confronted with the faces of their victims, it was impossible for most U-boat crews to show anything other than compassion. The U-boat war was a controversial war in that it centred on attacking merchant ships crewed largely by civilians. The enemy would argue that these ships were an integral part of the Allied war machine and therefore legitimate targets. This might suggest that Merchant Navy seamen were active servicemen in the practical sense of the word. No wonder it became known as *The Silent Service*.

The morning after the sinking of the *Tuscan Star,* Gordon Gill's energy was restored thanks to a breakfast of liver sausage, bread, marmalade and coffee. He was also handed 50 cigarettes. U-109, on the other hand, was virtually running empty, with only 33 cubic metres left in its tanks it would soon be ordered home. A refuelling stop was arranged on the way but the ambitious coordinates given by BdU, just south of the Canaries, were at the absolute limit of their range.

The following morning, Bleichrodt recorded his annoyance at the decision to send them home:

Heinrich Bleichrodt (U-109) – KTB U-boat Diary:
08.09.42   FF 1282   10:02
BdU-FT: Return voyage (*to Lorient*) started via DS30.
Commander: This radio message is just unbelievable. Just when I believe we have found the Allies main transport route, we have to leave the area. The given target can hardly be reached with the remaining fuel. We have to sail on the open Atlantic

Matters became even worse for the frustrated commander when he contacted BdU and asked them to reconsider its decision. The reply was not what he was hoping for:

BdU: FT 1236/8 U-109. Ensure you return to DG50. No prior refuelling possible.

The meeting point, DG50, was even further north than DS30. Bleichrodt was exasperated by this message but there was little he could do to change the decision, so U-109 was forced to continue its slow crawl towards Cape Verde. The crew attempted to conserve fuel by limiting diving drills and by moving fuel around the boat's tanks.

Just over two weeks after they left Oban, the slow moving convoy OG89 reached the Azores on the 15th September and, as planned, the *Peterton* dispersed and began its independent voyage to Buenos Aires. The first few days alone were potentially the most hazardous.

2nd Officer G. D. Howes: We proceeded until the 15th September, when off the Azores we broke Convoy, continuing independently for Buenos Aires

The seven torpedoes fired at the slippery *Ocean Might* had left U109 with only six torpedoes, making the boat sit much higher in the water than normal and when the north east trades winds stiffened on the 16th September, the larger profile presented by the boat served to delay the boat's progress even further by acting as an unwanted wind-brake. There was real concern they would not even make Cape Verde, let alone the Canaries.

SS Peterton shared none of these problems and was making steady progress southwards. The islands of the Azores were soon out of sight. Captain Thomas Marrie had sailed on this route on his previous voyage and was well aware of the threat posed by U-boats. However, the lack of U-boat reports led him to believe the danger was over. He shared his thoughts with his 2nd Officer:

> *2nd Officer G. D. Howes:* We received no submarine reports and by midnight on the 16th September the Captain considered we were out of the danger zone.

The *Peterton*'s master elected not to steer a zigzag course but took the extra precaution of preparing the ship's jolly boat as a make-shift lifeboat.

> *J. A. Morley:* The Master spent his spare time preparing the jolly boat with provisions in the event that we'd have to abandon ship. It was eerie, almost like he knew something was going to happen.

The *Peterton*'s crew would soon have reason to be thankful for the master's diligence with the lifeboats.

(Left) *Heinrich Bleichrodt* (1909–1977): Commander of U-109
(Alan J. Tennent)
(Right) *Wolfgang Hirschfeld* (1916–2005): Radio Operator U-109
(Wolfgang Hirschfeld)

U-109 'Hunter': Photographed at its base in Lorient,
France in May 1941. (Bundesarchiv)

SS Peterton 'Hunted'.(Port View) 400.1 x 52.4 x 28.4 feet, (5,221 GRT): Carlton Shipping Company (R. Chapman & Son). Built in 1919 by Richardson, Duck & Co. Ltd, Stockton on Tees. Photographed in Cape Town, South Africa in 1935. (John H. Marsh Maritime Collection)

4

THE ATTACK

The following reconstruction of events is based on written accounts from several sources, including the *Peterton*'s second officer, George Denis Howes, U-109's radio officer, Wolfgang Hirschfeld, and its commander, Heinrich Bleichrodt, and a series of interviews with Able Seaman Jack Morley between July 2004 and January 2010.

2nd Officer George Denis Howes (inset) made two reports, one for the Naval Control Service, in Freetown, in November 1942 and the other, following an interview with the Shipping Casualty Division, on the 8th January 1943, some four months after the sinking. As might be expected, this has resulted in one or two errors. No attempt has been made to change his original interpretation of events; they are only highlighted with comments. In addition, names of personnel, mentioned only by rank have been added for clarity.

SS *Peterton*'s movements are reconstructed from shipping movement cards, official log books, crew lists and correspondence maintained at the National Archives in Kew.

17 September 1942

On the morning of the 17th September 1942, Commander Heinrich Bleichrodt's main priority was U-109's desperate fuel situation and its imminent rendezvous with fuel tanker U-460.

They had burned up 97% of their fuel reserves, but Bleichrodt knew from experience not to run his tanks completely dry in the event of an emergency. Primarily, this meant the ability to fire up the diesels in the event of attack, but it also meant they could take on an enemy target should they sight one.

The weather was fine, with a bright sun providing good visibility. The sea was relatively calm and the wind blew only lightly. Shortly before midday, U-109's lookouts sighted mastheads directly astern. Although this meant the boat would have to make a complete about-turn, taking them even further away from their rendezvous point, an unescorted Allied freighter, travelling at little more than 8 knots, was a tempting target.

Bleichrodt recorded his frustration at the timing of the sighting of the enemy freighter in his diary. With mixed feelings, but driven by a sense of duty and fearful of reprisals, he ordered the attack:

> *Heinrich Bleichrodt (U-109) – KTB U-boat Diary:*
> 17.09.42   EH 3256   10:53
> Mast tops, steamer starboard – ahead in sight.
> *Commander:* Just now, when every drop of fuel is needed for our voyage to the meeting point with SCHNOOR (*U460 – Milch Cow Tanker*), we have to have a steamer (*Peterton*) cross our path. But with 8m^3 we can still do quite a bit.

The *Peterton*'s youngest apprentice, Teddy Hyde, had been assigned look-out duty and had scaled the rope ladder tied to the forward mast mainstays, up to the crow's nest located a few feet from the top of the forward mast. He was unaware they were already being observed through the periscope of a submerged U-boat.

Wolfgang Hirschfeld (U-109): The steamer was steering south-south-west at 10 knots. Within an hour we were submerged and awaiting her approach.

Bleichrodt was a cautious commander and although the *Peterton* was sailing right into the cross-hairs of his periscope sight, he made a verbal note of its armoury in the event of a counter-attack:

Wolfgang Hirschfeld (U-109): I heard Bleichrodt say: 'He has two guns astern by the look of it and several Oerlikons.'

Bleichrodt announced his decision to use three torpedoes. This excessive choice of violence was motivated by his perilous fuel situation, knowing he could ill-afford to miss his target and initiate a chase that might burn up the last of his fuel reserves. Neither could he afford to chase a damaged vessel. His attack had to be a hammer blow.

Commander Bleichrodt recorded the attack in his diary:

Heinrich Bleichrodt (U-109) – KTB U-boat Diary:
17.09.42   EH 3258   13:14
Triple-fan fired – three hits. Steamer lingers into list portside, sinks deeper.

2nd Officer G. D. Howes: We proceeded without incident until the 17th September when at 0910, in position 19.33N 29.83W whilst steaming at 9 knots on a course South (True), we were struck by three torpedoes.

Wolfgang Hirschfeld (U-109): Two hours after we had first sighted the ship we fired three torpedoes at a range of 800 yards and hit her with all three.

2nd Officer G. D. Howes (Naval Control Service): Three torpedoes (were fired) all within 20 seconds at about six second intervals (*In his Sinking Report, Howes states that all torpedoes were fired within 60 seconds*). No tracks were seen.

2nd Officer G. D. Howes: The first torpedo struck on the port side in the engine room. It was not a loud explosion and I thought at first we were being shelled by a Raider. No flash was seen from the explosion but a large column of water was thrown up. The engine-room was completely wrecked and the engines stopped immediately.

J. A. Morley: I was working on the forecastle with a group of men when the torpedo struck. We had the anchor hauled up on deck and were repairing its shackles when the first torpedo struck.

There was coal everywhere. The explosion threw tons of coal into the air, which landed on hatches and beams causing them to collapse and buckle. The coal dust stuck to our faces and we looked like Kentucky minstrels.

We all remained surprisingly calm, fully aware that we had been torpedoed, and started making our way aft towards the lifeboats. It was then that the second torpedo struck the aft section of the ship.

One of the apprentices (Teddy Hyde) was in the crow's nest when the first torpedo struck. He was on his way down when the second torpedo hit and the resulting explosion threw him down onto the deck below.

When the first torpedo struck, Teddy Hyde's first instinct was to head straight for the ladder. As he was negotiating his way down, the second torpedo hit six seconds after the first. The vibrations from the explosion shuddered through the ship and up the mast, causing it to shake violently. Teddy was thrown from the ladder and plunged to the deck.

Jack Morley's testimony provided an insight into the intensity of the explosion, with mangled beams and tons of coal flying through the air, more than enough force to loosen the apprentice's grasp.

Barely a month later, an able seaman, known only as 'Benny', would lose his life in identical circumstances when *SS Scapa Flow* (formerly *Quien Sabe*, a Finnish ship that had been confiscated in the USA and entered into Allied service under a new name), was torpedoed seven days out from Freetown by German U-boat, U-134. Benny had been posted in the crow's nest, high up on the forward mast, when shaken off by the blast of a second torpedo strike. He landed on a cargo hatch, right in front of a group of men heading for the lifeboats, and died instantly.

> *J. A. Morley:* We continued onwards, undaunted, and joined a group of men launching the starboard lifeboat. As we were launching the lifeboat, the third and final torpedo struck the forward part of the ship.

> *Sydney Ludlam:* I was doing A. A. duties when the torpedoes struck.

Several of the ship's gunners ran to the aft of the ship to man the 4" stern deck gun but soon realised the hopelessness of the situation and ran back to the boat deck lifeboat stations. The first torpedo had already sealed the *Peterton*'s fate, destroying its engine room and killing all of its occupants: 2nd Engineer Robert Morrison Gardiner (50), 3rd Engineer Henry William Runnacles (49), 4th Engineer Walter March (20), Greaser Hugh Gray (50), Fireman James Green (20), Donkeyman George Johnson (25), and Canadian Fireman Ray Tennant (24).

> 2nd *Officer G. D. Howes:* The port after lifeboat was blown overboard; No.2 derrick had jumped out of its crutches and was hanging over the ship's side. The bridge appeared to be undamaged but the deck was buckled and resembled a corrugated iron roof. Two further torpedoes struck the ship, one forward and one aft, both within a minute of the first explosion. The ship was enveloped in coal dust and it was impossible to see what damage had been caused. She

listed 45° to port and, thinking she was going right over, the Captain ordered abandon ship.

The heavy list adopted by the *Peterton* made it impossible to launch the port lifeboats and greatly hindered the crews' ability to get the starboard boats away.

J. A. Morley: When we reached the boat deck, one of the starboard lifeboats was already being lowered into the water by a couple of the lads. Once in the water we slid down into the lifeboat using the lifeboat's ropes.

2nd Officer G. D. Howes: We carried four lifeboats. The two forward boats were kept in the chocks, not swung out. The starboard after boat was lowered with difficulty, owing to the heavy list, and most of the crew abandoned ship in this lifeboat.

Three men remained onboard, the master and the two Marconi radio officers: 1st Radio Officer Jonathan Davies and 2nd Radio Officer Alfred White, who were furiously sending out distress messages.

2nd Officer G. D. Howes: The wireless operator sent out five distress messages and at 09:15 jumped overboard with the Captain as the ship heeled right over to port.

The *Peterton* was only seconds from going under and 2nd Radio Officer Alfred White was still onboard:

J. A. Morley: We saw poor Alfred standing on the poop deck looking down into the water. We shouted for him to jump but he just stood there, paralysed, just staring at the water below him. He wasn't wearing a life-jacket and couldn't swim. He went down with the ship.

2nd Officer G. D. Howes (Naval Control Service): W/T Officer (2nd Radio Officer Thomas Alfred White, 30) lost his life by hesitating to jump into sea to swim to lifeboat which lay a little way off sinking ship; went down with it.

The *Peterton* slipped horizontally beneath the waves, turned bottom up and sank. After twenty-three years of trusty service for R. Chapman & Son, its proud career was over and it plunged to the bottom of the North Atlantic with its cargo of 6,000 tons of coal, finally settling at a depth in excess of 4km, far out of the reach of man and the submarine that sent it there. It had become the final resting place of the seven men from the engine room crew and the 2nd Radio Officer.

2nd Officer G. D. Howes: We collected the men from the water and found we had 36 (*Actual number was 35*) men in the lifeboat. When the ship sank, No. 2 lifeboat, which had been resting in the chocks, floated off. The Chief Officer (Francis Fairweather, 42, East Ham) saw this boat in the water, dived overboard and swam to it to see if it was seaworthy.

When he got there, he found two men already bailing out the lifeboat:

J. A. Morley: George Norfolk turned to me and said 'We're going to get that boat'. As I dived in he shouted: 'Watch out for sharks!' When we reached the Jolly Boat we saw it was full of water so we climbed in and started bailing. I looked up and saw the U-boat approaching the starboard lifeboat. Her guns were manned, so fearing the worst we ducked down into the bottom of the Jolly and dared not show our faces.

Wolfgang Hirschfeld (U-109): We surfaced and approached the lifeboats which were stable, well equipped and capable of reaching the Cape Verde Islands. The ship's master was asked to identify himself.

2nd Officer G. D. Howes: The Submarine Commander asked the name of the Ship, and on being told, he asked for the Captain. The Captain, instead of keeping quiet as we had suggested, spoke up and consequently was taken prisoner. The Commander then asked for the Chief Engineer (Thomas Cuthbert Gorman, 44, N. Shields) but this man had no intention of spending the rest of the war in a concentration camp and promptly said he had gone down with the ship. We were asked if we had plenty of water, and given the course and distance to the Azores *(U-109 gave them a course to Cape Verde).*

Captain Thomas Marrie had ignored the advice of his crew by announcing his identity to the crew of U-109. He knew as well as they did that it was the policy of U-boat commanders to identify and arrest senior officers of merchant vessels. So, why was he so impulsively honest?

On approaching lifeboats, U-boat commanders usually took the precaution of ordering the manning of their guns in the unlikely event of survivors putting up resistance. This had the effect of making survivors, already shocked by the attack and the rapid loss of their ship, even more fearful. Many had heard or read stories of U-boat commanders ordering the massacre of survivors, although the only confirmed reports revealed that these kinds of atrocities were only ever committed by Japanese U-boat commanders. The rumours of massacres were far from the truth, but the average Merchant Navy seaman was not privy to Kriegsmarine Commander Dönitz's policy for handling survivors. Using a megaphone, U-boat commanders would normally ask the officers to identify themselves. Overcome by shock and the stress of having guns pointed at them, it is not surprising that survivors usually answered questions willingly. Captain Thomas Marrie was no different in this respect. Even if officers were calm enough to keep quiet, U-boat commanders usually questioned the other lifeboat occupants until they got the answers they were looking for.

Equally as important to U-boat commanders, was to determine the name of the ship, cargo and where they were bound. This information was very useful to BdU. From the name of the vessel they could look up its tonnage and add it to the 'profit and loss' account. From the description of the cargo they could build up a picture of the materials the Allies were trading. The intended destinations of merchant vessels would be used to facilitate more effective placement of U-boats in the Atlantic.

Although most survivors routinely gave up this information, some had the nerve to give misleading answers or worse: The Radio Operator of the *Tymeric*, sunk by a U-boat on the 23rd November 1940, told its commander to 'Go to Hell'. The survivors from SS *Scapa Flow* even felt sorry for the German U-boat men, describing them as 'poor cunts' because they had to live and fight in an 'undersea coffin'. All 48 hands in U-134 perished in their so called undersea coffin when it was sunk off the coast of Spain on the 24th August 1943.

According to Wolfgang Hirschfeld, Captain Thomas Marrie was carrying a pouch containing secret course instructions to Freetown, which he subsequently handed over to the commander of U-109. This is in conflict with the 2nd Officer George Howes' assertion that:

> 2nd *Officer G. D. Howes:* All confidential books and wireless books were kept in weighted boxes and went down with the ship

Marrie could have concealed any remaining ship's papers in the lifeboat or thrown them overboard if he was that concerned about the contents of the pouch falling into enemy hands. So what did he hand over? The answer to this mystery probably lies in Heinrich Bleichrodt's War Diary. It is highly unlikely that a coup, such as the acquisition of secret papers, would have been omitted. Bleichrodt's KTB for the patrol on which the *Peterton* ship was sunk mentions the ship's papers but the word 'geheim' (secret) is not there, so it is probable that no secret papers were included. Even routing instructions, if they were general enough, would not necessarily be a breach of security. Any course instructions may also have been just for that one ship and therefore useless to German intelligence. The logical conclusion is that the ship's papers were far more harmless than Hirschfeld thought.

Captain Marrie was escorted below deck and introduced to U-109's other prisoners, Captain Norman Ross Caird and Gordon Gill. Regaining his composure somewhat, he could not resist a dig at his captors and told them he was pleased they had wasted three torpedoes on his old ship and added that if they had failed to sink them he would have destroyed U-109 with his Oerlikons. Caird expressed his personal relief that Marrie's plan had failed.

2nd Officer G. D. Howes: After being alongside for 3 or 4 minutes the submarine steamed off and was not seen again.

Heinrich Bleichrodt entered *Peterton*'s details into his KTB and notes that the captain had some papers with him.

Heinrich Bleichrodt (U-109) – KTB U-boat Diary:
EH 3,258 br D Peterton 5,221 BRT+9+/34x /
5,758 tons coal – Buenos Aires
Commander: Approached lifeboats. Took the captain on board with papers.

2nd Officer George Howes did his best to remember the U-boat's identifying marks but failed to identify it as German. If he had asked, they would have most likely told him, just as they did for the survivors of the *Tuscan Star*, sunk only nine days earlier:

'Tell your government you were sunk with the compliments of U-109!'

2nd Officer G. D. Howes: The Submarine appeared to be a newish ship. She had a shield vertically striped with the three Italian colours, red, green and white and with some sort of crest in the centre, painted on her conning tower. There was a gun about 8 feet forward of the conning tower and another one aft. I did not see any gun on the conning tower. She had single jumping wires on each side. The Commander was a clean-shaven, fair man of medium build, dressed in a khaki shirt and no hat; he spoke with a German accent I only saw a few of the crew, these men had dark complexions, I think they were Italians. They were dressed in blue shorts and singlets.

2nd Officer George Howes believed he had spoken to U-109's commander, but Commander Bleichrodt wore a full beard, so it is more likely the survivors had spoken to his colleague, Lt. Schramm.

It seems somewhat strange that Howes mentioned the German accents and yet, at the same time, believed it to be an Italian submarine. Taking into account the considerable stress both he and the surviving members of the crew were under, it is hardly surprising his thoughts were jumbled.

Eventually, U-109 steamed away leaving the bewildered crew of the *Peterton* to fend for themselves.

> *J. A. Morley:* We were mightily relieved when the U-boat motored away. The starboard lifeboat rowed over to us as we continued to bale the jolly. We were all in a state of shock but there were no tears, no screaming, not even from the apprentices.

> *2nd Officer G. D. Howes:* After the Submarine had disappeared we rowed over to the Chief Officer. He told me that No. 2 boat was leaking slightly but that he could take a few men. I gave him 11 men, making 23 in my boat and 12 in No. 2 boat.

> *J. A. Morley:* We just took the men as they came, there was no selection process. However, George Norfolk was quite insistent that the boat took no more than 12 men – he said 13 was an unlucky number. It was quite cramped, as our boat was much smaller than the starboard lifeboat.

Once U-109 was out of sight, the men finally took stock of their situation:

> *J. A. Morley:* We realised that some of the men had gone down with the ship but it was only after things had settled down that we were able to identify them. Canadian, Ray Tennant (24), was among the dead. He was a good friend. Charlie Smith (19) was particularly upset, as he and Tennant were great pals.

We all lived in the same street in Hull. We accepted that loss of life was fate; there was little you could do about it. The men were quiet but got on with what they were doing. Our minds soon turned to thoughts of rescue.

The survivors in the starboard lifeboat harboured similar thoughts of rescue but it would be some time before their wish was granted. They had some sailing to do.

A series of telegrams sent by British Authorities in Freetown and Buenos Aires, obtained from the National Archives, revealed how the men were distributed between the two lifeboats.

Starboard Lifeboat

HOWES, Second Officer
GEORGE DENIS
Hull, Age 43

THOMPSON, Third Mate
ERNEST BENJAMIN
Norfolk Age 32

GORMAN, First Engineer
THOMAS CUTHBERT
North Shields, Age 44

DAVIES, First Radio Officer
JONATHAN ISLWYN
Goodwich, Age 30

NOCK, Able Seaman
FRANCIS
Hull, Age 20

RICHARDSON, Greaser
ALBERT
Hull, Age 39

WATT, Bosun
JOHN
Lerwick, Age 59

OSBORNE, Fireman
SAMUEL
Hull, Age 31

PENNINGTON, Sailor
GEORGE THOMAS
Wigan, Age 19

CHAND, Fireman
HATI
Trinidad, Age 24

ENNIS, Sailor
JOHN
Wexford, Age 27

SWAN, Steward
ARCHIBALD MORRISION
Sunderland, Age 33

THIRKETTLE Cabin Boy
HAROLD DENNIS
Hull, Age 19

LAMBIE, DEMS Merchant Navy
W. E.
Bristol, Age 28

HARRISON, Mess Boy
REGINALD
Scunthorpe, Age 17

LEWINGTON, DEMS Army
ALBERT WILLIAM
London, Age 25

LUDLAM, DEMS Army
SYDNEY
Sheffield, Age 21

HICKLING, DEMS Royal Navy
ALBERT
Leicester, Age 35

HYDE, Apprentice
EDWARD BRIGGS
Cullercoats, Age 15

MINNEY, DEMS Royal Navy
RONALD,
Caterham, Age 21

MEEKS, Apprentice
JAMES NICHOLSON
South Shields, Age 15

FISHER, Cook
GEO
Sunderland, Age 32

Port Lifeboat

FAIRWEATHER, First Officer
FRANCIS BULLER.
East Ham, Age 42

NORFOLK Able Seaman
GEORGE RAYMOND
Hull, Age 27

MORLEY, Ordinary Seaman
JOHN ALBERT
Hull, Age 18

STEPHENSON, Ordinary Seaman
JAMES HENRY
Hull, Age 22

BYRNE, Galley Boy
MICHAEL
Goole, Age 17

KEAY, Sailor
GEORGE
Hull, Age 19

SMITH, Fireman
CHARLES EDWARD JOHNSON
Hull, Age 19

GOODFELLOW, Fireman
ALAN
Hull, Age 18

KEAY, Sailor
GEORGE
Hull, Age 19

LYTLE, DEMS Merchant Navy
WILLIAM
Belfast, Age 33

BROOKS, DEMS Merchant Navy
WILLIAM
Preston, Age 18

HAUGHTON, Fireman
WILLIAM
Methil, Age 22

U-109 in the Gulf of Guinea: Photographed only days before it sank, the *SS Peterton* on 17th September 1942. Tanned lookouts scan the horizon looking for masts. *(Wolfgang Hirschfeld)*

SS Peterton (starboard view): starboard-aft lifeboat which carried 22 of the crew for 49-days is visible to the left of the funnel. Its loss marked a welcome change in fortunes for Chapman of Newcastle during World War Two who lost no further ships to enemy fire. *(Library of Contemporary History, Stuttgart)*

5

LIFEBOAT VOYAGE

SS Peterton was one of 2,535 British merchant vessels lost in the North Atlantic in World War Two, contributing eight victims to the final death toll of 29,180. 1942 had been a terrible year for Allied shipping with 1,006 vessels (5.5 million tons), accounting for almost half of all shipping lost in the North Atlantic arena for the entire war. The death toll would have been even higher but for the fighting resolve of those individuals who found themselves adrift at sea in a lifeboat often thousands of miles from land in appalling weather conditions. Aside from the humane aspect, it was also vital for the Merchant Navy to recycle as many men as possible to help stem the loss of skilled labour required to maintain Britain's merchant fleet. Over 50% of all survivors were picked up by rescuers within one day and could be quickly repatriated and allocated to another vessel; others were less fortunate and would spend weeks, and in some cases, months in lifeboats and rafts.

Following Captain Thomas Marrie's arrest and 1st Officer Francis Fairweather's transfer to the jolly boat, 2nd Officer George Howes took command of the starboard lifeboat. Unknown to him, and the twenty-one survivors crammed into the *Peterton*'s starboard lifeboat, they were about to embark on one of the most remarkable lifeboat voyages of the Second World War.

2nd Officer George Howes stated that his lifeboat contained twenty-three men but most sources quote only twenty-two. The *Peterton*'s List of Crew indicates that they sailed with a crew of forty-three. When accounting for the eight fatalities, the transfer of twelve men to the jolly boat and the arrest of the Master, this leaves only twenty-two men. Perhaps the loss of the Master confused his count, or there were twenty-three men in his boat. Lists of Crew were known to be wrong due to occasional clerical errors. The quoted number of survivors has not been altered in the various sources in this book. The correct figure is assumed to be twenty-two.

Jimmy Meeks and Teddy Hyde remained in the larger starboard lifeboat together with their Geordie shipmates: Chief Engineer Thomas Gorman, Steward Archie Swan and Ship's Cook George Fisher, who must have regretted helping out his employer by joining the crew of the *Peterton* when they lost their previous cook.

Chief Engineer Thomas Cuthbert Gorman (inset) was born in North Shields on the 2nd June 1898. His Merchant Navy career had begun smoothly in the final year of the First World War and he had worked his way rapidly up to the position of Chief Engineer. However, his reputation suffered a blow when he was accused of negligence in an incident that resulted in the loss of *SS Knebworth* in June 1929. Whilst anchored off Point St. Martin in the Bay of Biscay waiting to enter port, *SS Knebworth* had broken anchor and drifted onto rocks where it subsequently broke in two and sank. One of its crew, Donkeyman Robert Tait, of Newcastle upon Tyne, was washed overboard and drowned. A formal investigation held at the Moot Hall, Newcastle-upon-Tyne, between the 22nd

and 27th May 1930, concluded that the disaster could have been averted had the ship maintained sufficient steam pressure to restart its engines once its anchor broke. The ship's Master had given his approval to allow the steam pressure to be reduced in order to repair a steam leak reported to him by Chief Engineer Thomas Gorman. It was claimed by the investigation panel that Gorman had contributed to the disaster by obtaining the Master's consent to reduce the pressure in the starboard boiler in order to repair a steam leak that was later considered by the investigation panel not to be urgent, and then by delaying commencement of the work. The ship's Master contributed to the disaster by not verifying the seriousness of the steam leak and by not leaving the anchorage position sooner when weather conditions were more favourable. Despite this early blot on his record, Thomas Gorman's career was not unduly affected and by 1942 he had put the accident behind him.

Of the Hull contingent only Frank Nock, Albert Richardson, Samuel Osborne and Harold Thirkettle remained in the starboard lifeboat. Frank Nock was a popular figure amongst his colleagues and his positive personality would prove as important to the morale of the survivors in the starboard lifeboat as George Norfolk's jokes were to the men in the jolly boat. Harold Thirkettle was brought up in one of Hull's poorer districts and frequently irritated his seniors, many of which declined to comment positively on his conduct in their crew reports.

Bosun John 'Jimmy' Watt (inset) was the oldest member of the crew at 59 years of age. Born in Lerwick in the Shetland

Islands, he was a veteran of the First World War, where he had been unlucky enough to be torpedoed on three occasions. His bad luck followed him into the Second World War where he had already been torpedoed twice and shipwrecked once. His last ship, *SS Derrymore* (4,799 GRT), was torpedoed on the 13th February 1942. Days earlier it had arrived in Singapore with 2,000 tons of explosives and crated Spitfire aircraft as deck cargo, but too late to prevent the fall of Singapore to the Japanese. They took evacuees aboard and sailed for Java with about 200 servicemen. They later joined up with *HMS Stronghold*, *HMS Jupiter* and four tankers but were torpedoed by a Japanese submarine (I-25) north-west of Java. Jimmy Watt was among the survivors rescued by *HMAS Ballarat*. Nine men were killed. It could have been considerably more had the torpedo not struck the only part of the ship not likely to cause a major explosion. Watt had, once again, dodged death.

DEMS gunners Sydney Ludlam (21) and Albert Lewington (26) occupied the starboard lifeboat. It was Sydney Ludlam's first voyage following the completion of his four months of initial training as an Army gunner. Later, his mother would express her anger and disgust that her son had been sent to sea after such a short period of training. This was normal for the time, and he had been paired with an experienced hand in Albert Lewington.

Aside from Irishman, John Ennis, the only other 'foreigner' in the starboard lifeboat was Trinidadian, Hati Chand.

Jack Morley tried to remember who had transferred to the port lifeboat:

J. A. Morley: If I recall, Chas Smith (19) Hull, George Keay (19) Hull, Jimmy Stephenson (22) Hull, Alan Goodfellow (18) Hull and Herbert Weaver (34) Hull, were among the men who joined our boat.

Despite Jack Morley's insistence that the port lifeboat was filled randomly, it is evident that the younger men from Hull instinctively preferred to stay together.

J. A. Morley: Fairweather was in charge of our lifeboat and dished out the rations. He was a very quiet and serious man, always thinking. He looked after his men. George Norfolk was a laugh-a-minute character – he could find a joke in almost every situation. Charles Smith wasn't a big lad (*he was 5' 7"*) but he loved a good fist-fight. George Keay was a good shipmate. He could look after himself and was actually a fisherman by trade. He was quiet in the lifeboat and never showed any signs of panic. Alan Goodfellow, a very tall and quiet man. He kept to himself, a bit of a loner but a decent kid. Jimmy Stephenson was a buzzer, never still, always working. Herbert Weaver? He was getting on a bit! (*"He was 34"!*). We had a young lad called Michael Byrne; he came from Goole and a DEMS gunner, William Lytle. He was quiet, the total opposite of me!

The following account of both lifeboat voyages is supported by extracts from 2nd Officer George Howes' official accounts, a diary written by the *Peterton*'s bosun, Jimmy Watt, who recorded events on scraps of newspaper and backs of envelopes for the duration of their voyage, newspaper reports, interviews with members of survivors' families, and many interviews with survivor Jack Morley.

September 17 – Day 1

As the crew of the *Peterton* prepared themselves for a long lifeboat voyage, they were not the only ones with problems. U-109's fuel reserves were practically exhausted and they could only creep northwards towards France, their diesels being used only to recharge the boat's batteries. Unless help arrived soon, they too would be sending out SOS messages.

> 2nd *Officer G. D. Howes:* We decided to stay in the vicinity until noon in case our distress message had been picked up. Some of the rafts had floated off the ship, so we collected the food and water off these rafts and divided it between the two lifeboats.

SS *Peterton*'s starboard lifeboat was a typical Class 1 lifeboat. Despite being approved for up to 36 persons it measured only 24 feet in length. As they numbered only 22, the men did have some room to stretch out and crucially, it also meant there were more rations to go round. Class 1 lifeboats were required by the Ministry of War Transport to carry 25 gallons (200 pints) of water. Records of previous voyages show that Captain Thomas Marrie was fastidious in his preparation and servicing of lifeboats. He carried out inspections on a weekly basis and recorded the details in the ship's official logbook. He had seen enough ships sunk by torpedoes to know not to cut corners when dealing with the lifeboats.

Despite the fact that the starboard and port lifeboats were crowded with survivors, 2nd Officer George Howes and 1st Officer Francis Fairweather, decided not to redistribute the men amongst the rafts that had floated free from the *Peterton*'s deck. They would be less comfortable crowded together in the two lifeboats but concluded, quite sensibly, that the sailing ability offered by these boats might improve their chances of survival.

Statistically, three out of four lifeboats reached safety inside the first week and, in peacetime, their rescue would have been pretty much guaranteed as they lay in one of the busy shipping lanes that routed around the Cape. However, war had made it necessary to divert shipping away from the African coast and further out into the Atlantic. This made rescue by another vessel less likely. Because of this, it comes as no surprise that Howes and Fairweather decided to put rescue in their own hands and attempt to reach land.

The important question was – where? The men had several alternatives. North to the Azores was the shortest route to land. They could also have tried for the islands of Cape Verde that lay slightly further away to the south east. The west coast of Africa and Brazil were ambitious targets, but both reachable given enough time. Howes consulted his Chief Engineer, Thomas Cuthbert Gorman, who was a skilled yachtsman. They quickly agreed to steer a course north for the Azores.

2nd Officer G. D. Howes: At 1300 *(3 hours after they launched the lifeboats)* we set sail in a Northerly course for the Azores, which I estimated to be about 250 miles away.

By setting a course for the Azores, they ignored the U-boat men's advice to head south-west for Cape Verde. This was a decision they would quickly regret.

2nd Officer G. D. Howes: We sailed North during the night but at daybreak on the 18th September we had made no headway and, could still see the wreckage from the ship all round us.

The north-easterly winds, prevalent off the west coast of Africa at this time of year, would make it very difficult for the crew to reach the Azores since the crew's lifeboat lay in the teeth of the wind. They were not the only crew to encounter this problem. *SS Scapa Flow* would be sunk only a few hundred miles further to the south (south of Cape Verde), barely a month after the *Peterton* was torpedoed, and its survivors would set a northerly course towards Cape Verde. They abandoned their attempt for the exact same reason. The U-boat men were right! Having patrolled the area for several weeks, they understood the currents and prevailing winds far better than the Merchant Navy men; after all, the north-easterly winds had been delaying their northerly progress for days.

Cape Verde is a series eight islands, stretching over several hundred miles of the Atlantic Ocean. If the *Peterton*'s survivors held their lifeboats on a steady south-easterly course, they might run into one of them. The islands of St Antao and St Vicente, lying to the north-west of the Cape Verde, are mountainous and visible from a good distance. The island of Fogo, one of a number of islands forming a 'catcher's glove' behind St Vicente, is dominated by a volcano measuring over 9,000 feet above sea level and can be seen from far out at sea. The *Peterton* crew might just get close enough to spot one of these peaks.

Whether they would run into any ships on their way to Cape Verde was difficult to gauge. In peacetime, the area around Cape Verde was normally busy with international traffic, but most ships gave Cape Verde a wide berth since it was Portuguese territory and suspected of being used by German U-boats as a base for their attacks. On the other hand, the Portuguese had some ships and there were fleets of small fishing boats which worked out of the Cape Verde Islands and they were often seen over a hundred miles out. They might hope to see one of these boats, if only they could get close enough to the islands. 2nd Officer Howes and Chief Engineer Gorman felt they had no other option due to the prevailing winds but set a course for Cape Verde.

> 2nd *Officer G. D. Howes:* We decided to sail South East 1/2 East for Cape Verde Island, distance 250 miles. There was a light North Easterly wind and the weather was fine and clear.

1st Officer Francis Fairweather, sailing not too far away in the port lifeboat, came to the same conclusion but elected not to share his thoughts and plans with the occupants of his boat, other than to say they should try and sail towards land. Privately, Fairweather did not fancy their chances of reaching land and chose not to elaborate or worry the men unnecessarily. The circumstances of their sinking and acquisition of the port lifeboat meant he was without charts, sextant or compass and not in a position to promise the men anything.

J. A. Morley (Jolly Boat): We had no navigational equipment whatsoever! Fairweather told us nothing, we just assumed we were heading towards land.

Navigational charts were essential for any lifeboat expecting to reach the safety of land by sail or other means. At the beginning of the war, the standard routine relied on transferring charts to lifeboats when abandoning ship. This was far from practical and, in October 1942, and too late for the *Peterton*'s crew, a set of Admiralty charts was published specifically for lifeboats. The Master was carrying some documents but these had been confiscated by U-109.

Charts were of little use without a compass and sextant. These, too, were not standard lifeboat equipment and survivors were reliant on items like these being transferred when abandoning ship in the same manner as the radio and receiver. Also, there was not enough navigational equipment for more than one lifeboat, which caused problems when boats became separated. So, even if the starboard lifeboat had carried charts, the jolly boat would have been forced to navigate without charts. Some crews fabricated their own crude sextants using whatever materials they had at hand. The problem was not resolved during the war even though proposals, such as miniature sextants, were offered to the Ministry of War Transport for evaluation.

September 18 - Day 2

J. S. Watt: Midnight to 9a.m. lay repairing sail. Issued first rations – chocolates, biscuits, water. Broadcast SOS.

As the most senior officer, 2nd Officer George Howes was in charge of the starboard lifeboat and dictated the size and issue of rations. Bosun Jimmy Watt was entrusted with issuing these rations, this task being a natural extension of his normal role on the ship. It was his sixth time in a wartime lifeboat and he knew the drill well!

The initial quantity of water in the starboard lifeboat was the only factor Howes knew with any degree of certainty. How much rainfall they could expect was difficult to estimate, although he and Gorman must have had some idea, since they both had sailed down the West African coast on the *Peterton*'s previous voyage. That voyage had taken them as far south as Takoradi, Ghana, in the Gulf of Guinea.

The Ministry of War Transport realised quite early on in the war that lifeboat provisions were inadequate and improvements were necessary to increase the number of survivors that could be reassigned. In a search for improvements, they began, in the first half of 1941, by initiating an investigation into the adequacy of food and water supplies carried in lifeboats. At the time, most lifeboats carried ships biscuits, condensed milk and corned beef and the general opinion of survivors was that they were inadequate, particularly as all these foodstuffs promoted thirst. Nutritional and medical experts were equally critical of the provisions provided, so the Ministry approached food manufacturers and challenged them to develop some better alternatives. Malted milk tablets manufactured by Horlicks had already been in existence since 1940 and they were favoured ahead of condensed milk as they provided more nutritional value for less weight.

Both of the *Peterton*'s lifeboats were provisioned with a tinned meat product called Pemmican. Based on a traditional North American Native recipe of fat and dried meat, it had been developed by Bovril as a high-energy survival ration for use on Arctic and Antarctic expeditions and later as a lifeboat ration. It held a love-hate relationship with the survivors forced to eat it. The *Peterton*'s crew were reasonably positive:

> *2nd Officer G. D. Howes:* We found the food quite good and no one complained, one or two men could not eat the milk tablets, but I received no complaints about the Pemmican.

> *J. A. Morley (Jolly Boat):* It (Pemmican) was nothing special, we spread it on the biscuits – at least you felt you had eaten something. It's tasted a bit like Marmite.

Their colleagues from sister ship, *SS Earlston*, offered a different opinion when Pemmican was served during their lifeboat voyage:

> The Pemmican made several men sick when first issued and they refused to eat any more of it.

By the time the *Peterton*'s survivors started their voyage in 1942, Britain's manufacturers were already making lighter and more durable biscuits with a greater fat content. Chocolate manufacturers too had improved their products to make them less thirst inducing. By the summer of 1941, the Ministry of War Transport (as it was by then known) was able to issue a new schedule of lifeboat rations, which amounted to 14oz for each man the lifeboat or raft was certified for. The space saved by using higher energy rations was used to triple the water ration to 112oz which, according to a paper produced by the Royal Navy's Director-General of Medical Services, Surgeon Rear-Admiral Sheldon Dudley in January 1942, was the only ration that mattered. Food, he maintained, was only necessary for psychological reasons. In other words, a man could live off his fat. There was no mention of how long a boy could live off his fat.

In a guide produced by the Medical Research Council Committee on the Care of Shipwrecked Personnel, published at the beginning of 1943, called *A Guide to Preservation of Life at Sea after Shipwreck,* the recommendation was to issue 18oz (<1 pint) per man per day until 20oz remained and then drop down to 2oz per day.

Sleeping arrangements were a problem on both lifeboats:

J. A. Morley (Jolly Boat): Owing to the lack of space in our jolly boat, which was much smaller than the starboard lifeboat, we were forced to sleep in shifts. We curled up in the bottom of the boat or along the sides, it was cold and we dozed for a couple of hours at best. The starboard lifeboat had thwarts (transverse planking) about 6ft wide, so the men in that boat could lie across them to sleep.

The starboard lifeboat was larger but there were more men onboard and, therefore, sleeping room was just as limited as in the jolly boat, so a shift system similar to that of the jolly boat was put into use.

J. A. Morley (Jolly Boat): I wasn't prepared for a long open lifeboat voyage dressed only in a pair of khaki shorts. I became very cold at night.

We washed ourselves in seawater and if anyone needed the toilet they probably went at night, as I can't recall anyone doing their business during the day. Anyhow, we didn't have much to pass due to our restricted rations.

We used the water in our tanks sparingly just in case we were in for a long ride. 1st Mate Fairweather issued the water ration in a small beaker that hung from the water tank on a chain. One beaker in the morning and one at night.

2nd Officer G. D. Howes: We had to guess the time for rationing out the water by looking at the Sun.

2nd Officer George Howes' immediate priority was getting SOS messages out to ships that might have been in the area. He was far from certain anyone could hear them!

2nd Officer G. D. Howes: We had the boat's Wireless set in my boat and transmitted each morning, and night. As we had not time to get the receiving set off the ship, we did not know if our messages were being picked up.

An effective radio transmitter was a Ministry of War Transport innovation that enabled survivors to contact nearby ships and alert them of their location. In 1941, in consultation with the International Maritime Radio Company, the Ministry of War Transport developed a water-tight battery powered radio transmitter that was claimed to have a range of 200 miles and could be packed down in a small suitcase. The smaller receiver was carried over the shoulder on straps. In June 1941 it became a requirement under merchant shipping rules to carry such a set. Unfortunately, the crew of the *Peterton*, like so many other crews, left behind the smaller receiving set so they never knew if their messages were being heard.

September 19 – Day 3

> *J. S. Watt:* Decent sailing breeze. All well onboard. Broadcast SOS morning and evening.

September 20 – Day 4

> *J. S. Watt:* Stopped to repair sail and broadcast SOS. Fresh north-east wind, moderate swell.

U-109's fuel situation was perilous with only emergency reserves remaining. If they were not replenished by the same evening, they too would be under the power of sail. U-boats had the ability to erect sails but sailing them was no laughing matter, as Wolfgang Hirschfeld noted in his diary. The problem was that the supply boat U-460 was not answering their calls. The crew of U-109 were afraid Commander Schnoor's boat had been sunk and if that were the case they would have been in serious trouble.

U-460 finally made contact at 20:00 hours, and was welcomed with a mixture of relief and irritation. U-109 received 39 cubic metres of fuel and provisions for five days, enough to get them back to the U-boat pens in Lorient. At midnight, U-109 parted company with U-460. A refuelling operation left both U-boats vulnerable to attack, so they were both keen to finish the job and move on.

Heinrich Bleichrodt (U-109) - KTB U-boat Diary:
20.09.42   DS 1954   20:12
U 460 (Schnoor) in sight 21:00–00:30
Take-over fuel and provisions for 5 days.

September 21 – Day 5

J. S. Watt: Boat sailing fairly well.

J. A. Morley (Jolly Boat): We passed the time by talking about the different ships we had all sailed on and whether we would be rescued. Chas Smith and I had sailed together earlier in the war on a Norwegian ship to Cuba. Chas' best mate, Ray Tennant, was with us too. We had been hanging around Milford Haven dock, fishing off the quayside, when we were approached and asked if we wanted to join a Norwegian vessel, so off we went! The Merchant Navy took me all over the world – I remember a bloke at home in Hull telling me once to 'get a life'. I could only laugh and tell him that I had experienced more in one year in the Merchant Navy than he was likely to experience in a lifetime.

As well as chatting about their maritime experiences, the

men passed the time by making and playing games:

> *Sydney Ludlam:* We played cards with a pack made out of snapshots of New York and with dominoes made from bits of wood.

> *Jimmy Meeks:* We spent a good deal of time playing cards and dominoes made out of cardboard and paper.

> *2nd Officer G. D. Howes:* We made our own entertainment by having spelling bees and singsongs. We also made a pack of cards from picture post cards of New York harbour. We had one or two games of solo with them. Then one or two of the cards blew away and the game had to finish.

Many of the survivors were smokers and their meagre supplies did not last long.

> *Jimmy Meeks:* We had no cigarettes but some of the men discovered that the packing from their lifejackets made quite a decent smoke.

The lining in the men's lifejackets was a material called Kapok. Due to its high flammability Kapok was far from ideal, but merchant seamen still preferred Kapok-filled lifejackets over older lifejackets that relied on cork for buoyancy. A person jumping from a ship with a cork lifejacket occasionally suffered fatal neck injuries as the highly buoyant cork refused to submerge with the wearer of the jacket. This fact resulted in the introduction of the Kapok lifejacket in 1940. Kapok is an organic product of the Kapok tree (also known as Vegetable Silk or Java Cotton), the fibre is buoyant, light, insulating, and water-repellent and, as the crew of the *Peterton* discovered, a rather decent smoke. First marketed at the turn of the century, Kapok's flammability caused it to be banned from the market until ways were found to reduce the problem. By 1940 it was very much regarded as the standard material for lifejackets before being eased out by synthetic materials in the 1950s.

September 22 – Day 6

> *J. S. Watt:* Sailing close-hauled about south-east.

The north easterly trade winds were pushing the lifeboats towards Cape Verde. If Howes' calculations were correct, they might see Cape Verde in a day or two.

September 23 – Day 7
The superior sailing characteristics of the starboard lifeboat, and the skill of its crew, made it impossible for the jolly boat to keep up.

> *J. A. Morley (Jolly Boat):* We could not keep up with the starboard lifeboat. She was much faster with her sail up and if we had roped ourselves together we would only have held her back.

> 2nd *Officer G. D. Howes:* We kept with the Chief Officer's boat until noon on the 23rd September

(*Survivors in jolly boat claim they lost contact on the 20th September*) when I stopped the boat, rigged the aerial and sent out an S.O.S. Message. We set sail again at 14:00 and continued throughout the night.

Whilst the survivors from the *Peterton* were chalking up their first week in their respective lifeboats, the crew of U-109 was celebrating the news that their commander, Heinrich Bleichrodt, had been awarded the Knights Cross of The Iron Cross by Adolf Hitler: 'In grateful appreciation of your heroic participation in the struggle for the future of the German people.' A small banquet was held in his name, using some of the supplies given to them by U-460. Captain Thomas Marrie, Captain Caird and Radio Operator Gordon Gill were also in attendance.

September 24 – Day 8
A day that would bring vastly differing fortunes to the inhabitants of the *Peterton*'s lifeboats:

> *J. S. Watt:* Approx 4:00 sighted vessel. Burnt flares and smoke floats, but not seen.
>
> *2nd Officer G. D. Howes:* The port boat was out of sight. At 16:00 hrs we sighted a steamer about $2\frac{1}{2}$ miles distant, sailing on a course South-South-East (True). We burned 4 flares and several smoke floats, the yellow hood was rigged and we were using red sails. The steamer continued on its course and did not see us. It was dusk at the time and I think it was just too dark to notice the smoke floats and just too light

for the flares. I am of the opinion that the Steamer had sighted the port lifeboat ahead of her and was so intent on picking up the crew of this boat that she was not keeping a very good lookout in other directions.

Howes would later tell the Naval Control Service that the starboard lifeboat was not equipped with rocket flares which were available at the time and would almost certainly have drawn the attention of the *Empire Whimbrel*'s crew.

J. A. Morley (Jolly Boat): We were always hoping to be picked up and although one or two of the lads were a bit low at times, morale was not too bad.

It was late in the evening, almost dark, when we noticed a steamer heading straight for us. Had it been any later, they would have steamed right past us. The *Empire Whimbrel* had seen us before we had seen them.

Fairweather took command as the *Empire Whimbrel* approached. He warned us not to get over excited or exert ourselves too much. He was smart enough to realise we were weak and exhausted and likely to fall overboard if we weren't careful.

They pulled alongside our lifeboat and threw the scramble nets over the side for us to climb up. I had been sitting in the lifeboat for eight days and it took a great deal of effort to force my cramped legs up the scramble net. When I eventually hauled myself onto the deck of the ship my legs just gave way.

Several of *Empire Whimbrel*'s crew were

Cockneys and they were right pleased to have rescued us. We told them that there was another lifeboat in the area but the *Empire Whimbrel* was alone and unescorted and they were afraid to stick around for too long in U-boat territory.

If anyone deserved recognition for their efforts in our lifeboat, then it has to be George Norfolk. He was a born leader, one of the leading lights in our boat, nothing daunted him.

After a diet of Pemmican and biscuits, we were delighted when *Empire Whimbrel*'s cook made us an Irish Stew, it was a meal I will never forget. They then gave us a dose of Epsom Salts to help with our bowel movements!

After a few days we had recovered most of our strength. We were given clothes, Dungarees and sweatshirts, and started helping the *Empire Whimbrel*'s crew around the ship.

Disappointed at not being spotted by *SS Empire Whimbrel* and still with no sign of Cape Verde, 2nd Officer George Howes realised their trip might be a long one. Rationing would have to be tightened if they were to have any chance of survival.

2nd Officer G. D. Howes: We started off with 35 gallons of water in the lifeboat and all the usual food. I dealt out the rations and gave each man one large dipper of water three times a day, with three biscuits spread with Pemmican, 3 or 4 milk tablets and two pieces of chocolate. I kept this ration going until the

24th September, when, having seen one ship pass us I was beginning to think we might be in for a long trip, so decided to cut down the water ration. I put a plug in the bottom of the dipper making it two inches smaller and continued giving the crew three dippers each day.

September 25 – Day 9
The following morning the men in the starboard lifeboat spotted the abandoned jolly boat.

> *2nd Officer G. D. Howes:* On the 25th September I sighted a lifeboat about $1^{1}/_{2}$ mile to the Southward, I altered course, went alongside and found it was our port boat. This boat looked as though it had been recently vacated and I assumed that the steamer we had seen had picked up the Chief Officer and his crew. We took all the food and water from it which luckily for us had been left behind, and on the Chief Engineer's suggestion I also took the sails and oars as well. The chocolate had been finished but there was still some Pemmican, biscuits and milk tablets left and a small amount of water. We were exceedingly thankful for these rations as ours were beginning to run dangerously low.

The point at which an individual's water ration becomes dangerously low was something the Ministry of War Transport was keen to find out. An examination of lifeboat and raft voyages between 1940 and 1944 established that a daily water ration of 4oz ($^{1}/_{5}$ pint) seemed to be the absolute minimum for long-term survival during lifecraft voyages. When daily rations dropped below this value, voyages over a month suffered a 90% casualty rate.

The water acquired from the abandoned jolly boat was a Godsend for the men in the starboard lifeboat but the relatively high number of men in it put them at a huge disadvantage. Howes and the Bosun, Jimmy Watt, would still have to be extremely careful with their water rationing – too much and they would run out before reaching land; too little and they would die anyway.

U-109 was just south of the Azores, heading towards the Bay of Biscay and the crew's minds were filled with thoughts of home, when its lookouts spotted the mastheads of a tanker heading east towards Gibraltar. They gave chase for several hours but high seas, and concerns about fuel, forced them to abandon the chase, thus denying Captain Thomas Marrie the dubious honour of witnessing a torpedo attack at first hand. Bleichrodt recorded the non-event in his diary:

Heinrich Bleichrodt (U-109) – KTB U-boat Diary:
25.09.42   CE 9984
15:28   Mast tops, Tanker in sight – in front
16:00   Tanker moves out of sight in rain storm
17:00   Abandon search because of fuel

September 26 – Day 10

J. S. Watt: Making little headway, apparently drifting. Sent SOS. Have no receiver on board. Lay all night anchored to sea.

2nd Officer G. D. Howes: On the 26th September the batteries of the Emergency Wireless failed and much to the disgust of the Wireless Operator (Jonathan Islwyn Davies, 30, Goodwich) I threw the set overboard, thus making a little more room for the crew.

Unlike American radios, British radios relied on battery power, which soon ran out. Problems with radios continued into 1944 but crews were occasionally rescued as a result of their distress messages being picked up, so most ships considered them worth the effort of keeping.

September 27 – Day 11

J. S. Watt: Fitted oar as aftermast and rigged spare sail. Increased speed and making good headway. Checked rations and stores. Have arranged to make same last 14 days and ration water to three times a day.

2nd Officer G. D. Howes: The Chief Engineer suggested we rigged an extra sail which we did, using an oar as a mast. We rigged a second jib using the second oar for a bowsprit. For booms on the sails we used the boat hook and wireless mast. If we had only had a good sailing breeze we would have made very good progress, but as it was we progressed very slowly, and at times hardly moved at all.

September 28 – Day 12
Heinrich Bleichrodt received some worrying news concerning fuel from one of his officers:

Heinrich Bleichrodt (U-109) – KTB U-boat Diary:
Commander: Schnoor claims to have supplied over 42 m³ but our own clock shows only 39m³.

Only 3 cubic metres of fuel; but it could make all the difference. Bleichrodt was furious at being short-changed by U-460 and blamed one of his officers for the oversight, although he reminded himself that the same officer had sometimes scrounged more than their allocation from other tankers. U-109 continued, submerged, heading north into the treacherous Bay of Biscay, surfacing periodically to recharge their batteries before diving again. Despite their cautious progress, it was not long before depth charges began to pound the boat, much to the consternation of Captain Marrie, Captain Caird and Gordon Gill, who were subsequently issued with lifejackets for their own safety.

October 5 – Day 19

J. S. Watt: Weather squally and heavy rain. Hauled down sail and collected rain water in two tanks (seven gallons).

Howes and Gorman realised they had missed the islands of Cape Verde. The winds and currents made it impossible to turn back and they would have to find another way of reaching land.

Unfortunately, there were very few alternatives. The prevailing north-easterly winds actually favoured a direct voyage to Brazil and a coastline they could not fail to miss, but the 2,000 nautical miles would take them a morale-shattering month at the very least. Howes and Gorman dismissed this option quickly as their food and water supplies would run out long before they sighted the Brazilian coast. Had they been alone in the lifeboat, and not sharing their meagre supplies with twenty hungry men, they might have considered this option more seriously. Even though the wind and currents did not allow them to set a direct course towards the West African coast, instead sending them on a south easterly course, they took solace in the fact that the coast was, at least, getting closer. The survivors from *SS Scapa Flow* would come to the same conclusion. At one stage, the *Scapa Flow*'s lifeboat had steered a course for Brazil, but several of the survivors were completely opposed to the idea and refused to work. Rough seas forced them to give up their attempt and, once the lifeboat was pointed east again, the morale of the men improved dramatically.

Since the starboard lifeboat contained no navigational equipment and their charts had been confiscated by the U-boat, Howes and Gorman did not know whether they would reach the west coast of Africa before supplies ran out. Their chances of running into a rescue ship would improve the closer they came to the coast so, for this reason, they chose to continue on the same south-easterly course, pushing their boat as far east as possible.

U-109 was met by a minesweeper escort and sailed into the U-boat pens at Lorient, jubilant at getting through the Bay of Biscay in one piece. They were met by a large cheering crowd and a barrage of photographers. Commander Bleichrodt was clean shaven and a band played as the men filed ashore with their three prisoners. Bleichrodt said his farewells to the captives before they were taken away by an armed guard and, as he did so, Captain Caird handed him a lighter and note on which was written:

> 'As a token of respect and admiration for Cdr. Bleichrodt, his officers and the crew of U-109. N-R Caird – SS *Vimeira*.'

October 7 – Day 21
Wolfgang Hirschfeld attended the Telegraphist's Debriefing Conference in Kernervel whilst the rest of U-109's crew were sleeping off their hangovers following their safe return to home.

U-109 Captives: Captain Thomas William Marrie (32), Sunderland (back to camera) talks to U-109's Petty Officer Otto Peters (second left), Gordon Gill (left), and Captain Caird (right). *(Wolfgang Hirschfeld)*

Jimmy Meeks also had something to celebrate, today was his 16th Birthday!

Jimmy Meeks: ... it was celebrated all right by eating two hard ship's biscuits.

Back home in Tyneside, his birthday was published in the Shields Gazette's Smiler Club column.

October 9 – Day 23

2nd *Officer G. D. Howes:* I rationed the biscuits to one a day, but continued on the same water ration.

October 13 – Day 27

J. S. Watt: The last of the Pemmican is eaten.

October 14 – Day 28

J. S. Watt: The biscuits and chocolate are finished leaving only malted milk tablets and water.

October 18 – Day 32

J. S. Watt: Rotten sailing weather until now but the crew are in good spirits.

Although the survivors still maintained hope of reaching the West Coast of Africa, they were, by now, actually sliding further away from the Continent as its contours began to turn eastwards, creating an angle that the lifeboat could not compensate for on its current south-south-easterly course. Each mile they sailed served only to send them further away from land. Had the lifeboat been equipped with navigational equipment, the men might well have chosen to stop sailing. Their only remaining hope rested on the increasingly unlikely event of being rescued by a passing ship.

October 20 – Day 34

> 2nd *Officer G. D. Howes:* From the 12th October until the 20th we lived on 8 milk tablets a day and 3 dippers of water. During this period we caught three small fish, the largest was only 7" long. These were divided into 23 pieces and so did not do much to lessen the pangs of hunger. We were hungry all the time and were always ready for our next meal, while the food lasted. We found the food quite good and noone complained, one or two men could not eat the milk tablets, but I received no complaints about the Pemmican.

> *Jimmy Meeks:* We fished most of the time, with improvised line and hook and when we caught the fish we just cut off their heads and ate them.

The occupants of Second World War lifeboats on longer voyages were able to improvise fishing tackle using safety pins and bent pieces of wire, but deep ocean fishing requires longer fishing lines. Even the most creative survivors were limited to catching shallow water fish and sea-life as they had little more than shoes laces or pieces of string to work with.

The occupants of the *Peterton*'s starboard lifeboat failed miserably in their attempts to catch food, only three small fish between the 12th and 20th October. The men in the port lifeboat caught nothing, despite having a career fisherman onboard (George Keay). There was no shortage of fish; they were regularly seen swimming around the port lifeboat, attracting the occasional shark.

The men could hardly be blamed; fishing equipment was not a regulation lifeboat issue. The Ministry of War Transport and, incredibly, the Norwegian authorities and Nortraships (The Norwegian Shipping and Trade Mission based in England that looked after Norwegian shipping interests), a body representing one of the world's largest fishing nations, failed to supply lifecraft with basic fishing equipment. It was such an obvious and glaring omission and one that would endure for the entire war. Many survivors were ignorant of the species of fish available and those that should be avoided. A booklet advising on the types of food available in the sea was suggested by survivors from previous lifeboat voyages. Able Seaman Johan Moe of *M/V Moldanger* put it perfectly:

'Food and fish swam around us without any possibility of catching anything. It was a perfect torture chamber.'

Survivors were left to experiment for themselves. The *Peterton*'s crew discovered that the barnacles growing on the bottom of their boat provided some nutrition, varieties of which taste like oysters. This was a fact lost on many boats.

Jimmy Meeks: The barnacles were quite sustaining.

2nd Officer G. D. Howes: I did not have any serious trouble with the men. After the 20th October when the food finished, they became very weak and were unwilling to do any work. It was very cool during the night but at midday the sun was blazing down on us.

Between the 26th September and the 20th October we experienced severe heavy rainfalls so were able to replenish the water supply. We collected the rain in the sail cover and bailed it out with empty tins into the water tanks.

October 21 – Day 35

2nd Officer G. D. Howes: Six of the crew became delirious during the heat of the day, the attacks seemed to start after the 21^{tst} October.

The heat of the day was in direct contrast to the long cold equatorial nights, made worse by the fact that most of the men were wearing the ragged remains of the light summer clothing they were dressed in on the morning of the sinking. Although this left them with little protection against the chilly, star-filled evenings, many of the men actually preferred nights, especially the early evening period when the air still held the warmth of the daytime sun and their thirst temporarily quenched by their bedtime water ration. There was little chance of being rescued at night, but a few hours respite from scanning horizons for rescue ships that never came was a welcome relief.

October 22 – Day 36

> *J. S. Watt:* Little progress today. Milk tablets finished.

October 23 – Day 37

> *J. S. Watt:* Checked water supply. Sufficient to allow three quarters of a gill three times a day. Crew still cheerful against these odds. Thank God!

October 26 – Day 40

> *J. S. Watt:* Just drifting. Hoping for the best. All the crew now feeling peckish, but just as cheerful as can be expected.

SS Empire Whimbrel arrived in Buenos Aires with Jack Morley and the eleven other survivors from the jolly boat. They were received by the British Authorities who immediately sent off a telegram to the British Admiralty informing them of the *Peterton*'s loss. The memo was forwarded to the Registry of Shipping and Seamen in Cardiff who had the job of informing the crew's families. In the memo, they advised the Admiralty that the *Peterton* had been torpedoed and sunk on the 17th September 1942 and that contact with the starboard lifeboat had been lost on the 20th September. They followed this with an additional telegram listing the members of crew who went down with the ship.

The *Peterton*'s owner, R. Chapman and Son, and the DEMS gunner's battery units, received copies of the telegrams and began to inform the men's families.

L/Bdr. Sydney Ludlam's family was sent the following telegram:

REGRET TO INFORM YOU
GNR LUDLAM S MISSING AT SEA 17/9/42 STOP
ANY FURTHER INFORMATION RECEIVED WILL
BE SENT TO YOU IMMEDIATELY STOP ++

The short telegram only mentioned that Sydney Ludlam went missing at sea on the 17th September. His poor family could be forgiven for believing their son was already dead since a month had passed since he was last seen. They were unaware he had been seen in the starboard lifeboat with twenty-one other survivors.

October 27 – Day 41

J. S. Watt: Poor sailing. Forced to tighten our belts

October 29 – Day 43

2nd Officer G. D. Howes: On the 29th October I reduced the water ration to two dippers a day, one in the day and one at night. When the men became delirious at midday I gave the worst ones an extra ration to bring them round. One of the Firemen saw this and pretended to be delirious (*Samuel Osborne and Hati Chand were the only Firemen in the lifeboat*) but I soon saw through that. The crew grumbled a bit about the cut in the water ration but none of them became troublesome. We used to wash our mouths out with salt water but no one drank any.

The crew had so far avoided drinking any seawater. It seems such an obvious thing to do but, surprisingly, according to Macdonald Critchley in *Shipwreck-survivors, a medical study,* published in 1943, it was the leading cause of death at high temperatures. The British Medical Council struggled to quantify the perils of drinking seawater, as it was not something that could be analysed in an experimental setting. However, experience from the First World War and statistics derived from the testimonies of survivors from the Second World War, made the message crystal clear, drinking seawater could only do you harm.

SS Lulworth Hill's carpenter, Kenneth Cooke was well aware of the dangers and noted during his lifeboat voyage:

'I caught some of the young boys sipping salt water (six of *Lulworth Hill*'s survivors were boys under the age of 18) and took the firmest action to stop the practice. During daylight I was able to exercise strict control, but under the cover of darkness there was little I could do.'

A British Medical Council study produced in 1956, entitled *The Hazards of Men in Ships Lost at Sea 1939 – 1944,* revealed that it took as little as three days adrift before some survivors began drinking quantities of seawater.

Although this study contains some minor omissions and discrepancies, it is a very comprehensive report and played a pivotal role in the development of new and improved lifesaving equipment in the post war years

Voyages where survivors drank only freshwater were ten times less likely to die than those who drank seawater. By the British Medical Council's own admission, these figures were difficult to rationalise because the amount of seawater the survivors drink was inversely proportional to the amount of freshwater a lifecraft possessed.

It is probably true to say that drinking seawater was the final act for many. As long as abundant supplies of freshwater remained no one would die of thirst. Once supplies diminished below the critical 4oz level, or ran out completely, then it was survival of the fittest, with the weaker willed succumbing first. Unfortunately, the crew of the *Peterton* were rapidly reaching this point.

> *2nd Officer G. D. Howes:* I drank the oil supplied to rub our feet and I believe it did me a lot of good. We saw a lot of sharks round the boat but even so we managed to have a swim on several occasions, keeping a good look out for the sharks. The men went over the side five at a time. We started off with 4 bottles of brandy in the boat. I divided 3 bottles amongst the crew, giving the delirious men an extra ration at mid-day, the 4th bottle I shared with the man at the tiller as we were doing most of the work.

October 30 – Day 44

> *J. S. Watt:* Little progress. Feel rotten about the men as have had to cut ration of water down to two a day.

October 31 – Day 45
Able Seaman Jack Morley could stop rueing his decision to leave *SS Reynolds* as it had gone missing on a voyage from Durban. Records from German U-boat U-504 state they intercepted a ship 210 miles from Durban on the 31st October 1942, hitting it with two torpedoes amidships and in the stern. The ship capsized and sank within a few seconds. It was claimed a few survivors, who were seen in the water, told the U-boat crew that their ship was the *SS Reynolds* enroute from Durban to India. The U-boat then left the scene and left the men to their fate. All forty-seven hands were lost.

November 1 – Day 46

J. S. Watt: Water getting low. Little wind.

2nd Officer G. D. Howes: By the 1st November we were all very weak. I still hoped to make land but was becoming rather downhearted. I put a larger plug in the water dipper and consequently reduced the water ration.

2nd Officer George Howes and Chief Engineer Thomas Gorman were, by now, very worried, but fully aware of the importance of maintaining morale amongst the crew – particularly its younger members. They chose not to broadcast their feelings.

November 2 – Day 47

J. S. Watt: Spirits getting low, too, but hoping for the best.

November 3 – Day 48

J. S. Watt: Will have to reduce water ration down to one a day tomorrow.

2nd Officer G. D. Howes: By the 3rd November I was becoming desperate with only 2$^{1}/_{2}$ gallons of water left, my daily consumption being $^{1}/_{2}$ a gallon. I told the crew that on the 4th November I should have to reduce the ration again and this idea was not received with much enthusiasm. From the 20th October onwards we did not have any rainfall, we experienced fair weather with very little sailing breeze and were not able to make a great deal of headway.

Nine survivors (7 Norwegians, a Dane and a Swede) from *M/V Moldanger* (6,827 GRT, Westfal Larsen & Co.), torpedoed on the 27th June 1942 by U-404 on a voyage from Buenos Aires to Brazil, spent 48 days adrift in conditions very similar to those of the *Peterton* crew. Able Seaman Johan Moe remembered their struggle to cope with their acute water shortage:

Our water ration was set to one glass a day 2dl (7oz). I can't say that thirst bothered me the first day on the raft because the hope of rescue was quite stimulating, but the thirst became worse as each day passed (*not surprising as they were drinking quantities below acceptable limits for long-term survival*).

The first storm did not come as a surprise. I saw it approaching gradually and it was no worse than it allowed us to collect some water. After the storm came the sun and for me started the real thirst with a dry mouth and throat. I did not expect us to deviate from the ration that was set at one glass of water every evening. At night I lay there with my own thoughts and many a time I saw a large glass of water in front of me and the painful wait to next evening and our water ration became a pattern for the day.

We had an insufferable thirst, and here we lay floating with water from horizon to horizon and could not drink a drop. I lay on my back and saw up at the sky from the horizon and thought, 'are we going to get another storm?' 'How will it go next time?' I sat up and like the others studied the skies and wondered if we were going to get rain. We got a shower and our tanks were full. How can you explain such a feeling? You began to think like a child.

Ship's Carpenter Kenneth Cooke on *SS Lulworth Hill* towards the end of his 50 day lifeboat voyage with 14 men:

'This was the beginning of the end, for thereafter death was in daily attendance on the rafts. Some died from the effects of drinking salt water; others were victims of the unremitting torture meted out by the elements, the merciless sun by day and the unrelenting cold at night. But in many cases it was lack of hope that killed. Physical fitness seemed to have little bearing on the sequence in which they died. Each time a man lost his faith in ultimate survival, he was doomed.'

If the crew of the *Peterton* were to avoid a similar fate, rescue would have to come very soon. Their chances were slim, still hundreds of miles from the safety of land and not a ship in sight.

> 2nd *Officer G. D. Howes:* I thought, if I have to die, I will die, but I don't want to go crazy and cause the others any trouble. I never mentioned it but perhaps others were thinking the same."

Hope was on the horizon. Their lifeboat had drifted in to an area of ocean patrolled by *HMT Canna*. The crew of the 545 ton armed navy trawler was used to keeping their eyes peeled for drifting lifeboats. On the 20th August 1942, they had picked up ten Norwegian survivors from the *D/T Mirlo*, 100 miles south west of Freetown. The lifeboat had sailed 770 miles following the loss of their ship to a torpedo fired by U-130 on the 11th August 1942. *HMT Canna* was one of three naval trawlers commissioned as anti-submarine warfare vessels, the others being *HMT Bengali* and *HMT Spaniard*. As well as anti-submarine duties, fishing trawlers like these were used extensively during the war on escort and mine sweeping duties since they were easy to convert for this purpose.

HMT Canna's triple expansion steam engine was only capable of 12 knots, much slower than type IXB U-boats such as U-109, which was capable of 18 knots. It was modestly armed, with only one 12 pounder and three 20mm AAs. Despite this, *HMT Canna* was an effective U-boat deterrent since no U-boat would dare risk an encounter that might leave even the tiniest of holes in its hull. *HMT Canna* was also carrying depth charges and could hunt submerged U-boats.

November 4 – Day 49

J. S. Watt: Little wind, crew getting exhausted.

In need of a miracle, and with the crew on their last legs, Seaman J. W. Hargreaves of *HMT Canna* spotted, in the distance, a small unidentified craft. He reported his sighting to *Canna*'s commander, Lt Bishop-Laggett, who promptly gave the order to approach.

2nd Officer G. D. Howes: On the 4th November at 16:00 I sighted a ship ahead of us. The crew seemed to come to life immediately and we raised a cheer.

J. S. Watt: Later sighted a ship. Boy, what a sight! Picked up at 5p.m. 430 miles approximately from West Africa.

Commanding Officer HMT Canna, Lt Bishop-Laggett: At 16:50 in 08.30N 20.23W *Canna* picked up 22 survivors from the *Peterton*. The lifeboat was sighted by Seaman J. W. Hargreaves when seven miles away. He can always be relied upon to keep a keen look-out.

2nd Officer George Howes' assertion that the crew 'waved and gave a cheer' was a remarkably restrained response in the circumstances, the men were simply too exhausted to fully demonstrate their proper emotions.

2nd Officer G. D. Howes: The ship – HMT *Canna*, came right alongside, none of us could walk so the crew of HMT *Canna* helped us on board. We were then in position 8.50N 20.42W. 420 miles West $^1/_2$ South of Freetown. Whilst in the lifeboat we had sailed 840 miles in 49 days.

Lying on the deck of the corvette, Sydney Ludlam asked if there were any Yorkshire men on the ship. A sailor replied: 'Yes, I come from Sheffield.'

It was only upon rescue that 2nd Officer George Howes received confirmation of something he had suspected for quite some time – that they had sailed many miles west of their initial target of Cape Verde, and that the coast of Africa had never been within their reach. They were extremely fortunate to run into HMT *Canna*.

2nd Officer G. D. Howes: We had sailed West of the Azores (*Howes probably means Cape Verde – The Azores was hundreds of miles to their north and well out of reach*) and consequently missed them. I do not think we should ever have reached land on the course we were steering owing to the strong current.

With the men safely onboard HMT *Canna* the rehabilitation process could begin.

2nd Officer G. D. Howes: HMT *Canna*'s crew looked after us very well – they had no doctor on board, but we received excellent treatment. The crew were given hot soup to drink but I preferred a weak brandy and water. After that the Chief Engineer and I had a hot bath, it was a slow process as we both had to assist each other to move about. After a cup of hot soup we went to bed and slept soundly. The following morning, although still rather weak I was breakfasting with the crew of the HMT *Canna* and eating the usual food.

Commanding Officer HMT Canna, Lt Bishop-Laggett: All of the survivors were emaciated, some extremely so and the greatest care had to be exercised to prevent injudicious feeding. In this I was ably assisted by the Chief Engineer whose concern for his men did not cease when they were rescued.

I consider the 100% survival of the men to be an extraordinary feat of endurance which must be constituted a record and that they did survive is entirely due to the untiring efforts of the Chief Engineer, Mr. T. C. Gorman and the 2nd Officer, Mr G. D. Howes. Those two officers, although having very little hope of survival, kept up the spirits of the others and never allowed hope to fade. They were the only two men capable of sailing the boat and by their leadership and example many valuable lives were undoubtedly saved.

2nd Officer G. D. Howes: Whilst in the lifeboat the Chief Engineer was outstanding and of great assistance to me. He made numerous suggestions which I carried out and found to be of great value. This man was a keen amateur sailor and was the only

man who took any interest in sailing the boat. Without him I should have had an extremely hard time. One of the Sailors, Nock (Francis Nock, 20, Hull), was also most helpful. He was always willing to do anything he could to help at any time when the rest of the crew were too tired to work.

Commanding Officer HMT Canna, Lt Bishop-Laggett: With the food found in the abandoned boat the 22 men had in all 70 lbs of food and 8 gallons of water and on this they survived for 48 days and 6 hours. The food average was an ounce per day per man.

On October 11th, they were reduced to 1 Horlicks tablet a day and these ran out on October 20th. Thus, when they were picked up they had nothing for 15 days excepting two small fish and some barnacles which they picked off the bottom of the boat.

J. S. Watt: I never gave up hope. I prayed to God for help. He sent help alright.

The starboard lifeboat's 49 day voyage was a remarkable feat of endurance and the survival of all of its inhabitants is largely thanks to the skill and experience of men like George Howes and Thomas Gorman. According to the British Medical Council's study of 1956, there were 764 recorded Allied lifeboat voyages undertaken in the Second World War and the voyage undertaken by the twenty-two survivors in the *Peterton*'s starboard lifeboat was one of only 164 boats and rafts which lasted longer than a week, and one of only forty-two that lasted more than fifteen days.

If the 12 pints of water available to each man in the *Peterton*'s lifeboat is spread over 49 days, it equates to only $^1/_4$ pint per man per day, barely over the 4oz critical value. The discovery of the port lifeboat on day 9 which contained a 'small amount of water', followed by heavy rainfall in the first few weeks – 7 gallons of water was collected on Day 19 alone – allowed 2nd Officer George Howes to supplement his supplies, so the daily water ration for each man was considerably more than the 4oz minimum. Although Howes gives no precise figures, Bosun Jimmy Watt recorded in his diary that following a check of their water supplies on Day 37, they had: *'sufficient to allow three quarters of a gill three times a day'*. This equates to a healthy 15oz per day, getting to the optimum 18oz per man per day. On Day 44 the ration was reduced in frequency to twice a day and also in quantity by plugging the dipper. So, by Day 49 the daily ration was down to $5^1/_2$ ozs per man per day, calculated from Howes' then daily consumption of $^3/_4$ gallon, which was barely above the 4oz minimum for survival.

The survival of the *Peterton* crew can be attributed to a combination of factors: being able to retrieve water from life rafts that had freed themselves from the ship's deck, the opportunity that the port lifeboat gave them to reduce the men onboard form 36 to 22 (lifeboats were frequently overcrowded as 50% of all ships sunk by torpedoes sank within 15 minutes and not all had the opportunity to redistribute survivors between boats), the discovery of the empty port lifeboat that the crew of their rescuers of the *Empire Whimbrel* had failed to sink, its water tanks and the rain collected in the first few weeks of their voyage. 2nd Officer George Howes himself believed that the discovery of the port lifeboat was the stroke of luck that ultimately saved them but he is doing himself a disservice because, even considering their luck with water supplies, without his cautious and disciplined rationing, they would not have survived for as long as they did.

In a paper produced in January 1942 by the Royal Navy's Director-General of Medical Services, Surgeon Rear-Admiral Sheldon Dudley, it was stated that men need over two pints of water each day in tropical climates to maintain a good physiological condition. The *Peterton*'s crew were not too concerned about maintaining a perfect physiological condition; had they done so they would have run out of water long before they were found. In his interview with the Naval Control Service, 2nd Officer George Howes suggested that lifeboats be fitted with a proper rain catching sheet. A decent idea which would allow them to leave the sail, normally used to collect water, on the mast where it belonged. Howes also suggested that the sail be yellow in colour in order to make them easier to spot by rescue ships. He also got it right by gradually reducing the daily water ration in the latter weeks of the voyage. With only 10 pints remaining onboard at rescue, 2nd Officer George Howes could hardly have judged it better, in a few more days all of the lifeboat's occupants would have perished. In this, he was both brilliant and lucky.

The three torpedoes used by U-109 to sink the *Peterton* was excessive for a vessel of its size and age and as a result, it sank in minutes, giving its crew little time to properly launch and man the lifeboats, a familiar pattern that often resulted in overloaded life crafts and compromised essential rations such as water. Water tanks were lost overboard or had their bungs knocked out in the process of launching lifeboats in such a short and chaotic period. The only logical solution to this problem was to find a way of allowing survivors to make their own water. As Dönitz began to position his U-boats ever further south in the Atlantic, the ability to produce water onboard a lifeboat became an issue that the Ministry of War Transport could no longer ignore as lifeboat voyages became longer and longer. In the preliminary paper produced by Surgeon Rear-Admiral Sheldon Dudley for the Ministry of War Transport in January 1942, it was proposed that the possibility for producing drinking water by distillation or chemical means should be investigated. The potential of distillation had already been demonstrated by the carpenter of the *Macon*, torpedoed 460 miles west of Madeira on the 24th July 1941. After the survivors had spent a thirsty week in their lifeboat, he suggested they try to make a still. Using a one gallon drum, a piece of tourniquet tubing from the first aid kit and a bucket in which a fire could be lit, they managed to produce a very impressive two gallons of drinking water, followed by a further gallon the next day. It took two years, and many more casualties, before the Ministry of War Transport (previously the Ministry of Shipping until 1941) made a firm decision to place distillation units in lifeboats as standard. Some shipping companies did provide them before the approved version arrived but others waited in case they wasted money on types that had to be replaced when approved ones finally arrived. The result was that during the two-year period that it took to process the approval of stills, many more sailors died unnecessarily.

Lifeboat equipment and provisions were never perfect but the improvements made by the Ministry of War Transport, particularly with regard to recommended rations, undoubtedly saved the lives of many of the *Peterton* crew. Had they undertaken the same 49 day voyage in the first two years of the war, they probably would have perished.

No matter how well a lifeboat was stocked, some ship owners and officers ensured their lifeboats were stocked with some extra treats like dried fruit and boiled sweets; it was inevitable that survivors on longer voyages were going to lose weight. How much weight did the *Peterton* crew members lose over 49 days? A comparison with the nine survivors from *M/V Moldanger* gives an indication. The Norwegian authorities, led by their Health Minister, were keen to carry out research in a move to improve the survival rates of their seamen. They recorded the weights of *Moldanger*'s survivors on rescue and then compared them with their weights when they were restored to full health. The Norwegians did not have the British staple Pemmican but were able to catch a number of large turtles and enough mackerel to give each man a daily ration of 3-4 fish for most of their voyage. Despite this, weight losses were still severe and varied between 28.5% and 19% for the nine survivors, with an average weight loss of 23.3%. 16-year-old Jimmy Meeks was of slim build and only 5' 3" tall and could not have weighed more than 9 stone at the beginning of his 49 day lifeboat voyage. A weight loss comparable to that suffered by the *Moldanger* survivors would have seen him shrink to 7 stone. It was likely that his weight was much less than this when rescued.

Of lifeboat voyages that exceeded 15 days, only ten lasted longer than the 49 days endured by the crew of the *Peterton*.

The longest lifeboat voyages of World War Two:

#	Ship	Sunk	Coordinates	Survivors	Deaths	Days	Craft
1	Fort Longueuil	19.09.42	10.00S/ 68.00W	2	5	134	Raft
2	Benlomond	23.11.42	00.30N/ 38.45W	1	0	133	Raft
3	Woolgar (Nor)	07.03.42	150nm SW Java	6	18	88	Boat
4	Zaandam (Holland)	02.11.42	01.25N/ 36.22W	3	2	83	Raft
5	Cerinthus	09.11.42	12.27N/ 27.45W	1	19	77	Boat
6	Etrib	14.06.42	43.18N/ 17.38W	1	Not Known	77	Not Known
7	Anglo Saxon	21.08.40	26.10N/ 34.09W	2	5	70	Jolly Boat
8	Tulagi	27.03.44	11.00S/ 78.40E	7	0	59	Raft
9	City of Cairo	06.11.42	23.30S/ 05.30W	2	15	52	Boat
10	Lulworth Hill	19.03.42	10.10S/ 01.00E	2	12	50	Raft
11	*Peterton*	17.09.42	19.20N/ 29.50W	22	0	49	Boat

Their lifeboat voyage was an extraordinary feat of endurance and is one of the most successful in terms of days adrift and number of survivors. However, one has to be cautious when comparing lifeboat voyages purely by days adrift. Some lifeboat voyages in the North Atlantic and Arctic Ocean lasted a matter of days but the icy temperatures ensured their occupants' experiences were no less heroic. The Medical

Council Report is very careful to pay great respect to external factors that can affect lifeboat voyages, in particular sea temperature, and tended to divide lifeboat voyages into categories based on the average sea temperature at the start point of the voyage: Less than 10°C, between 10–20°C and between 20–31°C. Only one voyage below 10°C lasted for more than 15 days.

These lifeboat voyages may be the longest recorded during the war, but in most cases they were at temperatures above 21°C. These voyages should therefore be regarded as the longest voyages in the Medical Council Report category 'C' (21–30°C). Voyages carried out in other (lower) temperature ranges should be grouped separately in order to assess them fairly. The voyage made by the *Peterton* crew is an epic in its own right but what makes it stand out compared to the ten lifeboat and raft voyages that were longer in duration, is the extraordinarily high number of survivors. Of the ten lifeboat voyages that exceeded 49 days, where survivor details are available, the combined total of survivors is only 27 against a combined total of 76 deaths. There is a clear transition from multiple survivors to the survival of a few hardy individuals and this appears to occur at or around the seven-week mark, when a lifeboat's original water supplies are exhausted and consumption outstrips what can be collected from rainfall. When a well-manned lifeboat's water supply falls below the lowest acceptable limit for maintaining life, death comes quickly. Bearing in mind that *Peterton*'s water supply was down to $2^{1}/_{2}$ gallons, and the men were already severely dehydrated, it is probably correct to assume that most onboard the lifeboat would have died within the next three or four days unless rain returned; although one or two hardy souls might have endured, no longer having to share the meagre water rations between 22 men.

It is rather disappointing that this story receives scant attention in Merchant Navy literature. A book was written about the ship *The City of Cairo* survivors' 52-day voyage: *Goodnight, Sorry for Sinking You, The story of the SS City of Cairo* by Ralph Barker. The survivors from *SS Lulworth Hill*, who spent 50 days adrift, received an entire chapter in Bernard Edwards' *The Fighting Tramps*, and also appears in detail in several other publications. The Norwegians from *M/V Moldanger*, who survived 48 days on a life raft, feature heavily in three Norwegian publications. So why is the *Peterton* survivors' story not recognised in the same way? If they were to feature in any book it should have been in G. H. Bennett's *Survivors – British Merchant Seamen in the Second World War*; yet they only received a brief mention in a section highlighting the advantages of having a skilled yachtsman in a lifeboat – in the *Peterton*'s case Chief Engineer Thomas Gorman. Not a great example of the advantages of having an experienced sailor onboard because, despite the Chief's best efforts, the winds and currents ensured that they never came close to reaching land. It can only be assumed that the omission of the *Peterton* is due to the fact that the men in the starboard lifeboat were too successful. In other words, no one drank seawater, or went mad and died. Their story may have been less dramatic in this respect but would it interest scientists looking for a blueprint for long-term survival in a lifeboat? The British Medical Council's study of World War Two lifeboat voyages: *The Hazards of Men in Ships Lost at Sea 1939–1944*, recorded the *Peterton*'s voyage in a chapter entitled *Some Interesting Voyages*, where the relative success of long voyages is discussed:

> Some of the long voyages were much more successful... One boat with 23 men onboard voyaged for 49 days, sailing 840 miles in a south-easterly direction from rectangle J6/2... The men were able to get some extra rations from another boat. They had fairly good weather and frequent squalls of rain.

Encouragingly, some consolation can be gained from the fact that an authority as respected as the British Medical Research Council recognised the *Peterton*'s starboard lifeboat voyage for the success it really was.

Lt. W. N. Bishop-Laggett, Commander Officer *HMT Canna*, was in no doubt that the abilities of Chief Engineer T. C. Gorman and 2nd Officer George Howes in maintaining morale contributed significantly to the survival of their men:

> *Commanding Officer HMT Canna, Lt Bishop-Laggett:* Those two officers, although having very little hope of survival, kept up the spirits of the others and never allowed hope to fade. They were the only two men capable of sailing the boat and by their leadership and example many valuable lives were undoubtedly saved.

The distinction of the longest lifeboat voyage made by a Briton in World War Two is held by 21-year old gunner Denis Whitehouse. He was one of only six men from D/S Woolgar (Norway) to survive an 88-day lifeboat voyage in the Indian Ocean. Eighteen other men perished during the ordeal.

West African Coast: U-109 torpedoed four ships south of Cape Verde before turning north for a planned rendezvous with U-460 to refuel. It ran into the southbound *SS Peterton* on the 17th September 1942 and sank it with three of its remaining six torpedoes. The starboard lifeboat drifted south-east and was picked up by *HMT Canna* 49 days later off Freetown.

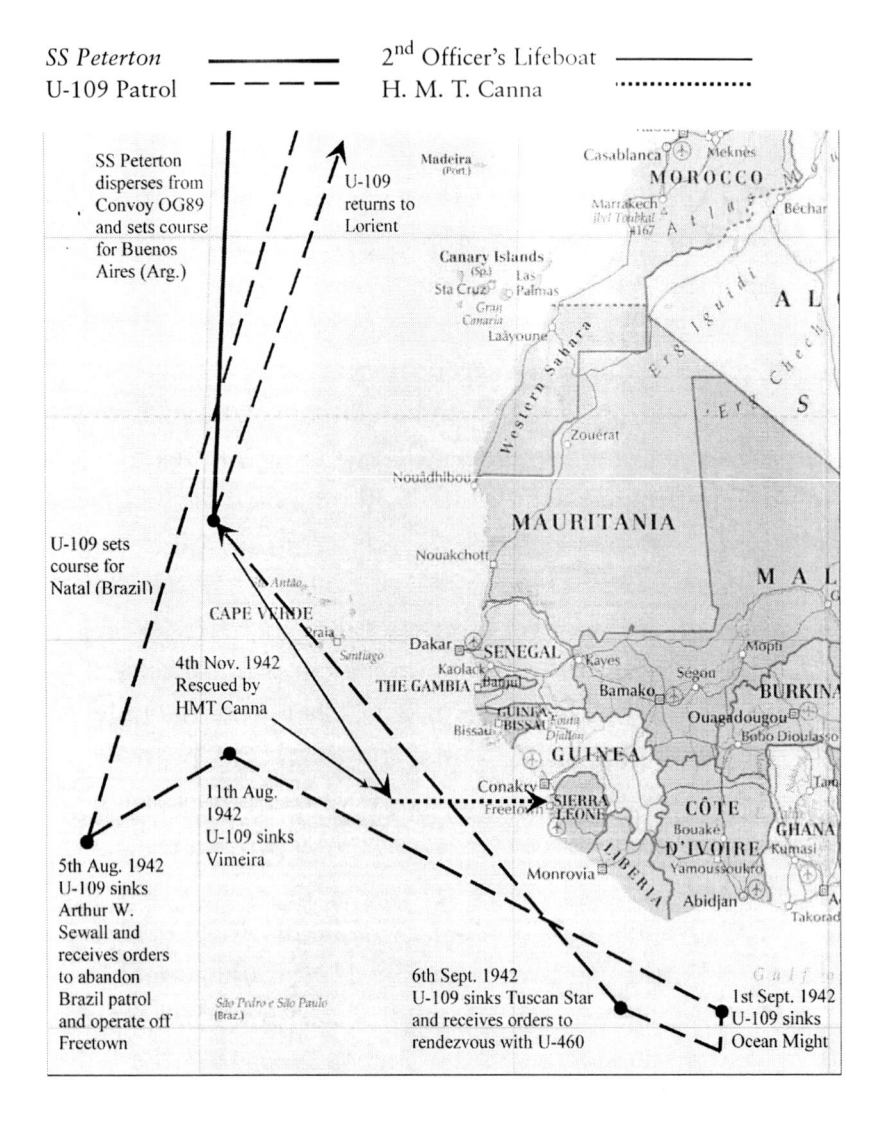

SS Peterton	————	2nd Officer's Lifeboat	————
U-109 Patrol	– – – –	H. M. T. Canna	············

SS Peterton disperses from Convoy OG89 and sets course for Buenos Aires (Arg.)

U-109 returns to Lorient

U-109 sets course for Natal (Brazil)

4th Nov. 1942 Rescued by HMT Canna

11th Aug. 1942 U-109 sinks Vimeira

5th Aug. 1942 U-109 sinks Arthur W. Sewall and receives orders to abandon Brazil patrol and operate off Freetown

6th Sept. 1942 U-109 sinks Tuscan Star and receives orders to rendezvous with U-460

1st Sept. 1942 U-109 sinks Ocean Might

The honour of the longest lifeboat voyage of World War Two goes to two Indians from SS *Fort Longueuil*, for enduring 134 days adrift, beating Chinese Poon Lim, the sole survivor from *Benlomond*, by one day. This rather flies in the face of many survivor reports written by officers, describing the lack of tenacity exhibited by Indian and Chinese 'lascars' in their lifeboats.

6

FREETOWN, SIERRA LEONE

SS *Peterton*'s survivors were severely weakened and emaciated following their ordeal but none more so than Teddy Hyde and Steward Archie Swan. Both men were critically ill and in need of urgent medical attention. Teddy, it must be remembered, had fallen from the ship's mast during the U-boat attack and suffered more than most during the lifeboat voyage. Archie Swan was no stranger to the sickbay having suffered from a hernia and malaria earlier in the summer.

Wasting no time, Commander Lt Bishop Leggett of *HMT Canna* plotted a direct course for the Allied controlled port of Freetown in Sierra Leone, on the west coast of Africa. It would also make repatriation that bit easier for the walking wounded since Freetown was a major staging post for Allied vessels arriving from South America, Australasia, Asia and the Gulf.

The port of Freetown had risen to prominence following the closure of the Mediterranean to Allied merchant vessels in June 1940 when Italy entered the war, resulting in the loss of the Suez Canal. Freetown had the best harbour on the West coast of Africa and was placed under the control of the British Army. As a Naval base, it served thirty-two separate convoy routes with facilities for bunkering coal and water. Although the area experienced high rainfall, water was sometimes in short supply and had to be shipped from the UK in tankers. Freetown was also a base for the Maritime Royal Artillery (MRA), the service that supplied many of the DEMS gunners aboard merchant vessels.

In the three days it took *HMT Canna* to reach Freetown, all but two of the survivors recovered sufficiently to be able to walk ashore: Teddy Hyde and steward, Archie Swan, were still too weak to walk and were carried ashore on stretchers.

The NCSO (Naval Control of Shipping Officer) in Freetown was informed of their arrival and sent a telegram to the British Admiralty listing the survivors, confirming their arrival in Freetown on the 7th November 1942. The memo was forwarded to the ships owners, R. Chapman and Son, the radio operators' employer, Marconi International, and the DEMS gunners' battery units. The men still did not know the fate of the jolly boat's survivors and the NCSO sent a memorandum to the Admiralty listing its occupants. Shortly after, several of the jolly boat's homeward bound survivors arrived in Freetown. They soon bumped into 2nd Officer George Howes:

> *2nd Officer G. D. Howes:* They told me that the EMPIRE WHIMBREL had pickled them up at 17:00 on the 24th September. This ship had fired five rounds at the lifeboat in order to sink her, but as the lifeboat still floated they decided to leave it where it was and continue on their way to Freetown. If this lifeboat had been sunk I am quite sure we should not be here to tell the story. The food and water taken from this lifeboat enabled us to last out for at least another week.

During an interview with Jack Morley in July 2004, it became apparent he was unaware that their abandoned lifeboat had been plundered by the survivors in the starboard lifeboat. He confirmed that the *Empire Whimbrel*'s gunners had tried to sink their boat and agreed it was very fortunate they failed to do so.

2nd Officer George Howes also learned from the survivors of the port lifeboat that they had landed in Buenos Aires on the 26th October 1942. Ironically, reaching their original destination, but not in the way they imagined when they left Oban at the start of September 1942.

> *J. A. Morley:* When we arrived in Buenos Aires we stayed in the Hotel Brochard at first but, later, members of the British Community took us in and gave us lodgings. I ended up at a ranch miles outside of the city with William Lytle and spent my days riding horses and playing football with the gauchos. I knew a life in the Merchant Navy would lead me to unusual places but I never in my wildest dreams imagined this.
>
> I was in Buenos Aires for $3\frac{1}{2}$ months before being sent home via Montevideo on the *Highland Chieftain* (Royal Mail Lines). We were treated terribly on that voyage, sleeping in hammocks in the bottom of the ship and being refused permission to go ashore when we docked in Montevideo.
>
> We thought about the lads in the other boat and although we had not heard from them for some time, we never gave up hope that they would be rescued.

The *Empire Whimbrel* would not see out the end of the war. On the 11th April 1943 it had the misfortune to run into U-181, commanded by U-boat ace Wolfgang Luth and became one of its forty-seven victims. Luth would end the war as the German Kriegsmarine's second most successful U-boat commander. Sailing unescorted on a voyage from Buenos Aires to Freetown, the *Empire Whimbrel* was hit by two torpedoes off the coast of Africa. Once the survivors' lifeboats were safely clear of the stricken vessel, Luth attempted to sink it with his artillery. The first round fired from the new 37mm AA gun caused the barrel to explode, killing one of the gun's crew. The *Empire Whimbrel* was finally sunk with 20 rounds fired from U-181's deck gun. Its crew were later picked up by *HMS Wolverine* and *HMS Witch* and landed in Freetown. Unlike the crew of U-181, they suffered no casualties.

By the 10th November 1942, most of the crew's families had been informed of the fate of the men, for some it was relief that their loved ones were among the survivors and, for others, the horror of realising they would never see their loved ones again. Teddy Hyde's mother received the news with joy but her son was still seriously ill lying in the 51st General Hospital in Freetown.

Following their privations in the lifeboat, the survivors from the *Peterton*'s starboard lifeboat needed to exercise caution. Freetown was ominously known as 'the white man's grave', surrounded as it was by malarial mangrove swamps and blighted by regular outbreaks of disease. Although the quota of rations recommended by the Ministry of War Transport had been enough to keep the men alive long enough to be rescued, their resistance to illness had been severely eroded by prolonged malnutrition and vitamin deficiency. Lack of proper sanitation and a stifling climate in Freetown only added to their woes. The able-bodied survivors from the *Clan MacPherson*, who reached Freetown in 1943, were appalled by the conditions there and the care meted out to them. The Master reported:

> It is no exaggeration to say the Grand Hotel was absolutely filthy... The sanitary arrangements were appalling... For breakfast we were given half a sausage and a small piece of fried bread.
>
> The general feeling seemed to be that no one cared what happened to survivors, so long as they were not bothered by them.

Arnold Hague had this to say about Freetown in his book: *The Allied Convoy System*:

> 'Freetown was no more than an oversize native village, with neither sanitation, water supply, communications of any kind nor any facilities normally associated with a European settlement. Disease was endemic, the climate atrocious and particularly enervating to Europeans.'

The survivors were driven the short distance to Freetown's 51st General Hospital, located atop Mount Aureol in the southern district of the town, where it overlooked the peninsula and its docks. The hospital was staffed by British doctors and nurses of the West African Forces.

There, Teddy Hyde was diagnosed with pneumonia, a condition he developed towards the end of his lifeboat voyage as a result of prolonged exposure and lack of sustenance. His dwindling reserves of energy had left his immune system weak and unable to fight germs normally harmless to a healthy person. Antibiotics, used in treating bacterial pneumonia, had been around for several years but were not very effective and scarcely available before 1943, when new and improved production techniques made it possible to produce stronger drugs in much greater quantities. By 1944, antibiotic penicillin was used extensively to treat troops during the Normandy invasion; but it was too late for Teddy. His doctors had to rely on traditional methods of treatment.

On the 11th November 1942, with the assistance of a staff nurse, Teddy Hyde dictated a letter to his family from his hospital bed and signed it in his own hand. In it he reported that he was feeling better and hoped to be home by Christmas. Despite not feeling well he was still able to enquire if his brother William had passed his exams. Before the letter was sent, Captain C. E. Holden of the Royal Army Medical Core added a few lines at the bottom. His words pulled no punches and made it clear that Teddy Hyde's life lay in the balance. Barbara Hyde reacted like the good mother that she was and sent a telegram to her son wishing him all the best.

Five days later, and despite the best efforts of the medical staff at the 51st General Hospital, Edward Briggs Hyde lost his fight for life. He was 15 years and 225 days old and over 3,000 miles from home. His Merchant Navy career had lasted just 75 days – most of those spent in the *Peterton*'s starboard lifeboat in the Mid-Atlantic.

It is not entirely surprising that the courageous Teddy Hyde ebbed away in the stifling Freetown heat. Most of the British airmen stationed in Freetown contracted malaria during their time there and, on a voyage to Takoradi and Freetown earlier that year, several members of the *Peterton*'s crew, including Archie Swan, had contracted the illness. It was

51st General Hospital Freetown, Sierra Leone: Ward 26 *(Freda Laycock Memorial).*

Jack Morley, Estancia La Dorita, Buenos Aires 1942: The survivors from the *Peterton*'s jolly boat were taken in by the British community in Buenos Aires. Jack found himself on a ranch where he spent his days riding with the gauchos. *(J. A. Morley – Private Collection)*

51st General Hospital.
West African Forces.
11/11/42.

Dear Mother,

You will know I am in hospital, but I am feeling a lot better & hope to be soon about. and coming home again.

Hope you are all keeping well at home, and I hope Will passes his exam for the Air Force.

Good wishes for Christmas but perhaps I'll be with you. Teddy

I regret that Teddy Hyde is very seriously ill but there is still slight hope of his recovery. Everything possible is being done for his comfort.

C. E. Holden Capt. R.A.M.C.

Teddy Hyde's Letter from Freetown 1942: Written in the hand of the attending nurse and signed by 'Teddy', who is hoping to be home for Christmas. Captain C. E. Holden of the Royal Army Medical Core pulls no punches in his footnote. *(Isabel McGregor – Private Collection)*

51st General Hospital Freetown, Sierra Leone: West African Forces Medical Staff, October 1942. *(Freda Laycock Memorial)*

not a place for an extremely weakened fifteen-year-old boy suffering from pneumonia. Teddy's loss was an emotionally draining experience for the men who had spent 49 gruelling days together with him in the starboard lifeboat.

If there is any comfort to gain from Teddy's last days, it is in the knowledge that the 51st General Hospital was staffed by a large group of British nurses who had an excellent reputation for their persistent and sympathetic handling of patients. Teddy Hyde certainly did not die alone.

Teddy Hyde was buried in King Tom Cemetery located at the north end of the Freetown peninsula. His body rests there today in Plot 7, Grave E5. His mother, Mrs Barbara Hyde, was informed by the ship's owners of his death, which was also reported in their local newspaper.

> *The Evening News:* After enduring great hardships while adrift in an open boat for 49 days – 20 days without food and with only rain water to drink – a 15-year-old Cullercoats boy making his first trip to sea as an apprentice died a few days after being

landed on British territory.

He was Edward Briggs Hyde, son of Mrs Hyde and the late Mr Victor Hyde, of 69 Eleanor Street Cullercoats, who was so keen for adventure that he threw up a job on a Northallerton farm to go to sea.

He left home in August and the following month the ship in which he was serving was torpedoed. He was at first reported missing and believed lost at sea as a result of enemy action and then came the joyful news that he had been rescued and landed. This was followed four days later by the tragic news that his death had taken place. In the meantime his mother had sent him a cablegram in the hope that it would help him to recover more speedily from the effects of his privations, but it is not yet known whether this message was received by the boy.

The owners of the vessel have informed Mrs Hyde that her boy had failed to respond to treatment given.

Sadly, Barbara Hyde's prophetic words about never seeing her son again had come true. Unable to bury his remains or attend his funeral, she was forced to grieve without even a proper final farewell. Teddy's sister, Isabel, was still evacuated to her grandmother's house when she received the news of Teddy's death. She had never considered the possibility that her brother would fail to return.

Isabel McGregor: I couldn't believe it when I realised I would never see him again. I think Teddy was aware of the dangers at sea but I wasn't.

There was some good news to report though. The steward, Archie Swan, was expected to make a full recovery having responded well to treatment.

As each survivor was deemed fit enough to leave the hospital, he was transferred to the British survivors' camp where most shipwrecked seamen were stationed until their shipping company representative could organise a ship home. The camp was run by religious missions and situated in a school building that had been commandeered for the purpose. Survivors were given tropical clothes for use in Freetown and later European clothes for the voyage home. This facility had already been in use for three years of the war, which says something about the number of ships being torpedoed by U-boats off the coast of West Africa.

The twenty seven survivors from *SS Scapa Flow* arrived at the British survivors' camp in Freetown on the 1st January 1943 when the last of the *Peterton*'s survivors were leaving for home.

'Spareman' Lars Skattebol, SS Scapa Flow: Some of the survivors in the camp during our stay there had been out in boats as long as forty days before rescue; others had had it relatively easy, like us, or had had a breeze, having been adrift less than a week.

There were four or five different groups of survivors in the camp at Freetown whose ships had been torpedoed, singly, over a period of several weeks, by the same U-boat. After each torpedoing, the German submarine commander had brought his U-boat up to the group of survivors, and, after the usual questioning; as the submarine sped away he had waved his hand and called, in English: 'Remember me to Winston Churchill'.

The survivors from the five vessels sunk by U-109 on its sixth mission all eventually made it to safety. The thirty-six survivors from the Norwegian *Arthur W. Sewall* – built in Newcastle upon Tyne in 1926 – were picked up by the Greek *D/S Athina Livanos* on the 10th August 1942 and landed in Port of Spain nine days later. Eight of the survivors were British. The *Sylvia de Larrinaga* picked up a lifeboat containing sixteen men from the *Vimeira* after two days. Their elation at being rescued was short lived, as the *Sylvia de Larrinaga* was herself torpedoed a few days later. The unfortunate survivors from the *Vimeira* were forced to board a lifeboat for a second time in a week. They suffered for a further twenty-nine days before being rescued by the Norwegian steamship *Siranger*. The fifty survivors from the *Ocean Might* spent six days in their lifeboats before coming ashore at the fishing village of New Ningo in Ghana.

Despite having a number of women and children onboard, the survivors from The Blue Star Line *M.V. Tuscan Star* had relatively few problems. Except for the inevitable discomfort and occasional squalls and some showers of rain, the voyage of the Captain's boat was uneventful. However, they were relieved when, at about 15:00, they sighted a large steamer coming up from the south and altered course to cut it off and were duly sighted and picked up by the Orient Liner *Otranto*, employed in government service, at about 16:30, reaching Freetown the following afternoon. The other lifeboats also reached safety and eventually made it to Freetown. Whilst the men waited for the next convoy to take them home, they stayed in the Mission where they were fed and watered and given a bed for the night. The following morning they were issued with clothes and toiletries.

Nine men died when the *Tuscan Star* sank, it had been loaded with 7,500 tonnes of Brazilian beef. If ever a sinking defined the material profligacy of war, the loss of *Tuscan Star* and its cargo did it perfectly.

As well as being the date of the *Peterton*'s demise, the 17th September 1942 is historically significant for another reason. Following the ill-fated attempt by Werner Hartenstein in U-156 to rescue survivors from the *Laconia* troop ship, an action that prompted much scorn from Bleichrodt, Karl Dönitz fired off a new standing order to his U-boats on the 17th September 1942, prohibiting all efforts at rescuing members of ships that have sunk and forbidding attempts to pick up swimmers, or place them in lifeboats, or right capsized boats or to supply provisions or water. Gordon Gill of the *Tuscan Star* would certainly have perished had this directive been issued two weeks earlier because the crew of U-109, on hearing his screams, pulled Gill, blinded by oil, out of the water. The fact that this directive was issued only hours after the sinking of the *Peterton* probably made little difference to the eventual fate of Jimmy Meeks and his crewmates for the simple reason that the lifeboats were already fully provisioned with water and were unable to accept Bleichrodt's offer of supplies. It was this sort of compassionate behaviour exhibited by Bleichrodt that Dönitz wanted to stamp out. The directive would come back to haunt Dönitz later, as it formed the backbone of the case against him at the Nuremberg Trials for war crimes. The Judge ruled that the order was too ambiguous to be considered as a clear order to kill and as a result Dönitz escaped relatively lightly with a ten-year prison sentence.

British Naval Intelligence at the Operations Intelligence Centre (OIC) in England was responsible for gathering intelligence from survivors of U-boat attacks in order to assist in their tracking of enemy U-boat operations. A huge chart hung on the wall in the Submarine Tracking Room, a bombproof concrete bunker known as the Citadel, used expressly for this purpose. To this end, the most senior survivor of any merchant ship lost at sea during the Second World War was normally interviewed by the Shipping Casualties Section and a Shipping Casualty Report produced for distribution to the Commander in Chief of Western Approaches and the OIC. The responsibility for providing the Shipping Casualty Report for the *Peterton* fell to 2nd Officer George Howes. His observations were well meaning but not that helpful; he believed that they had been spoken to by the U-boat's Commander, describing a clean-shaven man; but Bleichrodt wore a thick beard, so it was probably Lt Schramm who had addressed them. He also believed that the U-boat crew was Italian. This was a common error because German U-boat crewmen were often short and stocky, not the tall blond Teutonic types most British seamen expected. U-boat crewmembers operating further south in the Atlantic were often heavily tanned, which only added to the confusion. Italian U-boats did operate in the area – *Leonardo Da Vinci* sank *Lulworth Hill* earlier that year.

2nd Officer George Howes surprisingly failed to identify the lighthouse emblem that featured on both sides of U-109's conning tower during their sixth mission. The starboard emblem can be seen on a photograph of the conning tower featuring Heinrich Bleichrodt, and the port emblem, less clearly, on a photograph taken from the U-460 during the refuelling operation on the 20th September 1942, both featured in Wolfgang Hirschfeld's book. Howes described a shield with the Italian colours of red, green and white. U-boats frequently changed emblems and used additional emblems for single missions that did not find their way into the record books; it is possible Howes saw one of these. The lighthouse emblems featured on the conning tower of U-109 have a history going back to 1924 when the Kyffhauser Association (Veteran's Association for WW I Soldiers) met for the first time. When Bleichrodt was honoured with the Iron Cross, this association adopted U-109 as its mascot and its emblems were painted on the conning tower. The widespread use of emblems by German U-boat crews greatly assisted British Naval Intelligence in their identification of U-boats. U-boat crews saw themselves as non-conformists and, like many sailors, were highly superstitious. They could not be dissuaded from their use. Most U-boats displayed emblems during the war, with war themes varying from objects such as swords and axes, to the humorous, such as Mickey Mouse and unflattering caricatures of Winston Churchill. Many U-boats were *adopted* by cities and towns in Germany before and during the war. Many of these boats displayed the crests of those same towns on their conning towers together with the main emblem for the U-boat. It was also common for the same emblem to be seen on many boats; often this was the flotilla or a class emblem. U-109 was part of the 2nd Flotilla and had the appropriate emblem for this. Their class was defined by the club symbol from a deck of cards.

2nd Officer George Howes fails to mention Jimmy Watt in his report but the bosun's normal ship duties clearly extended to the lifeboat voyage. Whilst Howes was ultimately responsible for the boat, he relied on Jimmy Watt to report on the status of food and water supplies and to issue rations to the crew. Later in the voyage Watt kept a much closer eye on their meagre supplies so as to prevent the more desperate members of the crew from stealing extra rations – this was a problem experienced by many crews, particularly on very long voyages.

2nd Officer George Howes stated in his report that their lifeboat had sailed west of the Azores:

> 'We had sailed West of the Azores and consequently missed them. I do not think we should ever have reached land on the course we were steering owing to the strong current.'

This is almost certainly a typing error; he must have meant that they had sailed west of their intended target, Cape Verde. He was right in one respect, that they would not have reached land, at least not for a very long time.

Wolfgang Hirschfeld's and 2nd Officer George Howes' accounts of the sinking of the *Peterton* concur on most points with the exception of the timing. This can be attributed to the fact that the clocks on the *Peterton* were set at GMT, whilst U-109 operated at local time. Both accounts agree that the attack occurred at around ten minutes over the hour.

One of the surprising aspects of George Howes' report, considering the carnage U-109 had left in its wake, is that the *Peterton* received no U-boat warnings:

'We received no submarine reports and by midnight on the 16th September the Captain considered we were out of the danger zone.'

SS *Peterton* had sailed to Freetown and Takoradi earlier that year as part of convoy OS29 and it is possible that the Captain Thomas Marrie's knowledge of the route and the lack of submarine reports led him to believe they were more or less safe. It made little difference though, as the *Peterton* was capable of little more than 10 knots and as unprepared as the crew of U-109 were to make an attack, there was only one likely outcome.

3rd Officer Ernest Thompson, and Chief Steward Archie Swan, reported to their rescuers on *HMT Canna* that they had noticed something they described as 'a sort of valve' in the deck casing that had the words 'Turn left to open, turn right to shut' (or similar words). This information was probably unhelpful in terms of gaining useful intelligence in the fight against the U-boat menace.

Following his capture, Captain Thomas Marrie discovered that being picked up by a German U-boat by no means guaranteed survival, especially when U-109 ran the gauntlet of the Bay of Biscay. However, he survived the journey and spent the remaining three years of the war in captivity. There he was allowed to broadcast a message to his family on German radio. The German Kriegsmarine captured over 5,000 Allied merchant seamen during the war. Their arrest was in direct contravention of the Hague Convention but the Germans were fully aware of the value of these men to the Allied war effort and they would not be released.

HMT Canna, Isle Class 2 Naval Trawler: No picture of this vessel exists. Vessel pictured is sister ship *Lundy* which was built to the same design. *HMT Canna* was launched 18th November 1940 by Cochrane, Holmes & Co., Selby. (545 GRT) 150 x 27.5 x 10.5 feet. Triple expansion steam engine and one single ended boiler. 850 IHP. 12 knots. Armament: 1-12pdr A.A., 3-20mm A.A. Complement: 40. Owned by the Admiralty.
Pennant No: T 161 (Signifying Netlayer and Tender).
(Unkown source)

There were some 32 POW camps, which held merchant seamen in Europe during World War Two. There were also numerous camps throughout Africa, Asia, and the Far East, as well as the prison ship *Altmark*, but only one camp was built specifically for merchant seamen and that was the Marine Internierten Lager, better known to its inmates as Milag Nord. The camp was situated at Westerimke some ten miles North of Bremen. Seamen were first held in the concentration camp at Sandbostel until they built their own camp, Milag Nord, between October 1941 and April 1942. Merchant seamen of all nationalities were held at Milag Nord and over 5,000 were held here at any given time. Tom Marrie would start his three years there in barrack seventeen.

The merchant men POW's were guarded by elderly and disabled German sailors and suffered the same privations as any normal POW. Many POWs felt that the British Government and the shipping companies showed too little concern for them and their dependants. In 1999, ninety two-year-old Thomas Marrie posted his Milag Nord experiences in the form of a long poem, on the Milag website *www.milag.org*

The most successful U-boat commanders of World War Two:

	Name	Ships Sunk	Tonnage	First Ship Sunk	Last Ship Sunk
1	Otto Kretschmer	47	274,333	04 Oct 1939	16 Mar 1941
2	Wolfgang Luth	47	225,756	18 Jan 1940	12 Aug 1943
3	Erich Topp	36	198,658	17 Jul 1940	03 Aug 1942
4	Gunther Prien	31	193,808	05 Sep 1939	28 Feb 1941
5	Heinrich Liebe	34	185,377	06 Sep 1939	08 Jun 1941
6	Heinrich Lehmann-W'brock	25	179,212	11 Dec 1940	09 Mar 1942
7	Viktor Schiltze	34	174,896	31 Oct 1939	29 Jun 1941
8	Karl-Friedrich Merten	27	170,271	22 Sep 1941	06 Nov 1942
9	Herbert Schultze	26	169,439	05 Sep 1939	12 Jun 1941
10	Heinrich Bleichrodt	27	158,967	15 Sep 1940	17 Sep 1942

These tonnage figures (and sometimes the number of ships sunk) are still being debated by historians.

7

LOCAL HEROES

News that Jimmy Meeks, Edward Hyde and George Howes were missing reached their families long before HMT *Canna* picked them up, so by the time news of their rescue arrived, they had already been given up for dead. The relief to the men's families was enormous. Unfortunately, for Edward Hyde's family, relief turned to grief when Chapman officials contacted them only four days later to give them the dreadful news that Edward had failed to respond to treatment and had died of pneumonia.

It is not clear how Jimmy Meeks and the rest of the *Peterton*'s crew returned to England, although it is known that they did not all travel together. Sydney Ludlam, for one, travelled later than the others. The Freetown to Liverpool convoys (SL series) were suspended at the time as Britain was concentrating its efforts on the North African campaign and the SL series would not resume service until February 1943, so they did not return as passengers in a convoy. It is possible they risked travelling with a 'fast independent' or more likely they were taken to Gibraltar on a Royal Navy vessel and joined a convoy for home from there.

On arrival in the UK, their heroic voyage came to the attention of the national newspapers. The *Daily Mail*

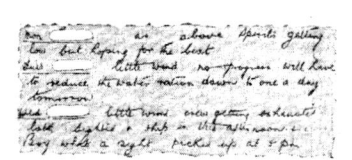

Empty Lifeboat Kept 23 Seamen from Death
By Daily Mail Reporter

TWENTY-THREE British seamen had drifted for eight days in an open lifeboat. Food and water were becoming exhausted. Across the sea bobbed another lifeboat. It was from their ship, torpedoed over carried a report about the men on the 10th December 1942 and included a photograph of Jimmy Watt giving a 'cheery wave'. Watt had every right to celebrate his survival; at 59 years old he was the oldest man onboard the lifeboat by over a decade and his survival can quite probably be attributed to the sheer ruggedness of the Scottish Islander.

Jimmy Meeks arrived on the doorstep of his family home in South Shields on the 7th December 1942, just in time for Christmas. According to his best friend, Bill Laybourne, Jimmy was remarkably silent about his experiences. When asked how his trip was, Jimmy's reply was brief and to the point: 'I was shipwrecked!'

His immediate concern was his lack of clothing. Although he had been provided with some clothing at the Mission in Freetown, his own clothing had gone down with the *Peterton* and the clothes he wore in the lifeboat were now rags. Suits were the attire of the day, and as Jimmy had no money to buy one, his friend Bill Laybourne kindly donated one.

According to the voyage ledger maintained at the Tyne & Wear Archive, Jimmy Meeks received a 'subsidence' payment of £7 7' for the period 7th December 1942 to 20th January 1943. Apart from a few months at the start of the war and contrary to popular belief, Merchant Navy seamen did receive a salary even after their ship was sunk. In December 1939, the Ministry of Shipping accepted a proposal from ship owners that survivors' salaries should continue for one month after the loss of their ship; or until they returned to the United Kingdom, whichever was the longer. Additional expenses were shared between the Government and the owners. Under these rules, Jimmy would have been entitled to pay from the 17th September 1942 to 7th December 1942. After the establishment of the Merchant Navy Reserve Pool in 1941, a survivor would receive wages while he was waiting to muster on his next ship, which explains the subsidence payment Jimmy received.

The cost of replacing clothing for survivors was a general grievance amongst Merchant Navy seamen and by March 1940, the Ministry of Shipping had established a government financed compensation scheme for officers and men. Masters could receive up to £100, £90 for certified officers, £50 for carpenters, £25 for seamen, greasers and firemen and £20 for boys, which was what Jimmy was entitled to. Proof also had to be provided that items were lost before any claim could be met.

Jimmy may have taken his experiences in his youthful stride but the local newspaper was impressed nevertheless: *The Shields Gazette and Shipping Telegraph* carried an interview with him.

> *The Shields Gazette and Shipping Times (January 1943)*: A Merchant Navy Apprentice James Nicholson Meeks, aged 16, has reached his home in Centenary Avenue South Shields. He was one of 22 members of the crew of a torpedoed ship who spent 49 days in an open boat.
>
> He told *The Shields Gazette* yesterday that they sucked barnacles off the side of the boat and ate raw fish to sustain them. He said that when picked up by a trawler and taken to Freetown South Africa they had only $1^{1}/_{2}$ gallons of water left, but all survived their terrible ordeal except Edward Hyde, another apprentice, of Cullercoats, who died in hospital later.

'We fished most of the time,' he said, 'with improvised line and hook and when we caught the fish we just cut off their heads and ate them. The barnacles where quite sustaining. We had no cigarettes but some of the men discovered that the packing from their lifejackets made quite a decent smoke.'

'After drifting for eight days we sighted a steamer and we fired flares to attract attention but they were not seen. We spent a good deal of time playing cards and dominoes made out of cardboard and paper'

Meeks said that after the ship had been torpedoed 800 miles from land, the submarine came alongside and the commander gave them matches and offered to give them water which they were unable to accept as the tanks were full.

Meeks is a member of *The Shields Gazette Smilers Club* and when the announcement of his 16th birthday was published in the Club column on October 7th he was in the lifeboat.

He was educated at South Shields High School for Boys and joined the Merchant Navy in September.

Jimmy Meeks received further recognition on the 6th July 1943 when his King's Commendation for brave conduct, was reported in the London Gazette. He was one of 2,568 merchant seamen to receive this award during the Second World War. In the same edition of the *London Gazette*, it was reported that 1st Officer Francis Buller Fairweather had also received a King's Commendation for brave conduct. 1st Radio Officer Jonathan Islwyn Davies received the same award.

2nd Officer George Denis Howes was awarded the George

Medal and Chief Engineer Thomas Cuthbert Gorman received an O.B.E.

Chief Engineer Thomas Gorman's reputation was now fully restored following the unfortunate incident earlier in his career where he unwittingly contributed to the loss of a ship and the death of a man.

London Gazette, Tuesday 6th July 1943: The Chief Engineer showed great courage and ably assisted the Second Officer. Towards the end, when there seemed to be little prospect of survival, Mr. Howes and Mr. Gorman never allowed hope to fade.

Able Seaman Francis Nock was awarded a British Empire Medal for his 'tireless efforts in the lifeboat'.

London Gazette, Tuesday 6th July 1943: Able Seaman Nock displayed courage and devotion to duty throughout and was of great help in the working and handling of the boat.

Edward Briggs Hyde received a posthumous King's Commendation which was also reported in *The Evening News* in Newcastle on the 7th July 1943:

The Evening News, Wednesday 7th July 1943
Cullercoats Apprentice Commended
A 15-year-old Cullercoats boy who died a few days after being landed on British territory after enduring great hardships while in an open boat for 49-days – 20 days without food and with only rainwater to

drink – had his name included in the latest list of Merchant Navy commendations.

He was Edward Briggs Hyde, apprentice, son of Mr Victor Hyde of 69 Eleanor Street, who was making his first trip to sea when the terrible experience befell him.

The Commendation for Brave Conduct awarded to Jimmy Meeks and Edward Hyde has its roots in the First World War as a semi-formal award similar to the Mention in Despatches, but the system was not formalized until 1939. Following the First World War, the gallantry awards system was adapted in recognition of the Merchant Navy's gallant acts in the face of the enemy. This position was achieved by recognising the fact that in times of war the Merchant Navy was in as much, if not more danger than the Royal Navy and that conditions were often indistinguishable. For this reason, Merchant Navy Personnel received Certificates of Mentions in Despatches during the Second World War. Furthermore they were entitled to wear their *Mentions in Despatches Emblem* for a King's Commendation for Brave Conduct.

Life, and particularly war, is full of ifs and buts. The injuries sustained by Edward Hyde were not immediately life-threatening which suggests that had help arrived sooner or had he transferred to the port lifeboat that was picked up only eight days later, he might have survived. It will never be known for sure, but the decision, or hand of fate, that resulted in him staying in the starboard lifeboat seemed the correct one at the time, it was larger, better equipped (the port lifeboat had no radio), didn't leak and seemed to offer the best chance for survival.

Jack Morley parents welcomed him home in January 1943, but they would not learn much about their son's exploits:

> *J. A. Morley:* I never told them! They knew I had been torpedoed but I was more interested in getting out and enjoying myself. I wasn't there long anyway before me and a few other lads from the lifeboat were sent to the Merchant Navy convalescent home in Limpsfield.

The Limpsfield convalescent home in Surrey was owned by The Merchant Seamen's War Memorial Society and was founded in 1920 by members of the National Union of Seamen (NUS) who recognised the need to provide the Mercantile Marine with facilities to 'care for injured and distressed seafarers'

Of the nine crewmen lost from the *Peterton*; seven are commemorated together with Edward Hyde at the Tower Hill Memorial on Panel 81.

GARDINER, Second Engineer Officer, ROBERT MORRISON, *SS Peterton* (Newcastle-on-Tyne). Merchant Navy. 17th September 1942. Age 50. Husband of Florence Gardiner, of Hull.

RUNNACLES, Third Engineer Officer, HENRY WILLIAM, *SS Peterton* (Newcastle-on-Tyne). Merchant Navy. 17th September 1942. Age 49. Husband of Lily Jane Runnacles, of Hull.

GRAY, Greaser, HUGH PATRICK, *SS Peterton* (Newcastle-on-Tyne). Merchant Navy. 17th September 1942. Age 50.

GREEN, Fireman and Trimmer, JAMES ERIC, *SS Peterton* (Newcastle-on-Tyne). Merchant Navy. 17th September 1942. Age 20. Son of Ernest and Jane Elizabeth Green, of Hull.

JOHNSON, Donkeyman, GEORGE, *SS Peterton* (Newcastle-on-Tyne). Merchant Navy. 17th September 1942. Age 25. Son of Henrietta Johnson, of Hull; husband of Margaret Johnson, of Hull. His stepbrother Richard also fell.

MARCH, Fourth Engineer Officer, WALTER, SS *Peterton* (Newcastle-on-Tyne). Merchant Navy. 17th September 1942. Age 20. Son of John Henry and Elsie March, of Hull.

WHITE, Second Radio Officer, THOMAS ALFRED, *SS Peterton* (Newcastle-on-Tyne). Merchant Navy. 17th September 1942. Age 30. Son of J. William and Emily Elizabeth White; husband of Ivy Marjorie White, of Cottingham, Yorkshire.

The eighth casualty, Canadian Ray Tennant, is commemorated on the Canadian, Halifax (Nova Scotia) Memorial, Panel 22:

TENNANT, Fireman and Trimmer, RAY, ALFRED *SS Peterton* (Newcastle-on-Tyne). Merchant Navy. 17th September 1942. Age 24. Son of Mr and Mrs George A. Tennant of Montreal, Quebec, Canada.

GVI RI

This scroll commemorates

E. B. Hyde, Apprentice
Merchant Navy

held in honour as one who served King and Country in the world war of 1939-1945 and gave his life to save mankind from tyranny. May his sacrifice help to bring the peace and freedom for which he died.

Commemoration Scroll: E. B. Hyde, Apprentice, Merchant Navy.
(Isabel McGregor – Private Collection)

8

THE SINKING OF U-109 AND THE END OF THE U-BOAT WAR

On the 8th January 1943, 2nd Officer George Howes was interviewed by a clerk from the Ministry's Shipping Casualty Division where he was able to report in detail the loss of the *Peterton* and the fortunate rescue of its surviving crew members.

Their rescuers, *HMT Canna* had not been so lucky. The 560-ton trawler was in Lagos Harbour, Nigeria, on the 5th December 1942, when an accidental spillage of petrol swamped the harbour and exploded destroying *Canna* and other ships nearby, including trawlers *Bengali* and *Spaniard*. Barely a month had passed since the *Canna* had picked up the exhausted survivors from the *Peterton*'s lifeboat. *HMT Canna*'s commander, Lt. W. N. Bishop-Laggett and Seaman J. W. Hargreaves, who spotted the *Peterton*'s lifeboat, survived the explosion as most of the crew were billeted onshore at the time of the explosion. Sub Lieutenant Jim Fowler, the sole survivor from another navy trawler – the Kelt, described the scene when *HMT Canna*, *Bengali* and *Spaniard* blew up:

> 'There wasn't a sound, they went up absolutely silently, bits and pieces shooting up into the air in front of me... There was a tremendous amount of damage to the dockyard, the main building 400 yards away being severely damaged at the entrance, and as

for the three trawlers, when I looked back they had vanished completely – they just weren't there.'

Jimmy Meeks did not like speaking about his war experiences and changed the subject whenever the topic was raised. However, one of the few and most surprising facts to emerge was that he was extremely keen to get back to sea. Only youthful exuberance can possibly explain his actions, for the North Atlantic was not a safe place at that time. Fortunately for Jimmy, the balance of the U-boat war was about to tip very much in his and the Allies' favour, being turned on its head in as little as eight weeks in the spring of 1943. Until then, the outcome had been very much in the balance. As early as 1940 convoy escort ships had been using centrimetric radar to detect surfaced U-boats. In October 1941, a high frequency direction-finding device was issued to them for the first time. The HF/DF, or *Huff Duff* as it became known relied on the U-boats' profligate use of radio to map their respective locations. These developments played key roles in reducing the effectiveness of Dönitz's U-boats, but to gain the upper hand in the U-boat war, the Allies realised that breaking the German Enigma code transmissions was a greater priority.

British Intelligence at Bletchley Park had been sporadically decoding German Enigma code transmissions from as early as 1940, but in June 1941, following the capture of U-110 (like U-109, also a type IXB) and its signal code books, the Allies were finally able to decode German transmissions at a speed that was operationally viable. The solutions to the Enigma intercepts were given the cover name *Ultra* by the British.

The Polish mathematician Marian Rejewski is credited with solving Enigma but to facilitate the large scale decoding requirements, the British built a number of mechanical computers known as *Bombes*. Although the introduction of a separate U-boat cipher key net in October 1941 put more strain on the limited sources at Bletchley Park, Ultra still remained Britain's greatest secret weapon of the war.

Then, on the 1st February 1942, Ultra was plunged into darkness when the German Kriegsmarine put into service a new Enigma machine, the M4. Using the U-boats own Triton key net, the M4 was an upgrade of the existing three-cogged machine, with a new additional fourth non-rotating rotor that increased the number of transmission code combinations by a factor of twenty-six.

Although the loss of Ultra was damaging, its presence would not have made up for the mistakes made by the US Navy when the Americans entered the war in December 1941. Two years of bitter experience had seen the British introduce much-improved tactics in their efforts to maintain supply links between Britain and the United States, such as the utilisation of convoys protected by destroyers and air cover where range permitted. The gap in air cover in the mid-Atlantic accounted for three of every four Allied ships sunk, such was the importance of air cover to convoy defence. By pushing the convoy route further north and creating air bases on Newfoundland and Iceland, the Allies were able to reduce this gap.

The Americans, by entering the war against Germany, opened the door to U-boat activities in their own waters as neutrality zones no longer applied. In January 1942, Dönitz launched Operation Drumbeat, sending his long range U-boats to the east coast of the United States. The Americans relative inexperience resulted in heavy losses off their east coast in the first six months of 1942. Their own merchant vessels often travelled alone, and often with their navigation lights blazing, making them vulnerable at night. At the same time, Admiral Ernest King, the overall chief of American Atlantic operations started to milk the Atlantic Fleet of their destroyers and other ships for use in the Pacific against the Japanese. He more or less abandoned convoys on trans-Atlantic routes to their own fate in American waters. He reasoned that: 'Inadequately escorted convoys are worse than none'.

At one stage, the Americans only supplied two per cent of the destroyers carrying out convoy protection duties.

Admiral King's actions were based on an ignorance of convoy tactics and to some extent his dislike of the British. Whatever the motivation, it was an act of negligence that nearly cost Britain the war. Convoys that had been escorted safely by British and Canadian destroyers across the Atlantic were subsequently massacred by the U-boats waiting for them in American waters. The Germans referred to this area of operations as *The American Turkey Shoot* and it led to what they would call their *Second Happy Time*.

It took some heavy lobbying by British Naval intelligence in March 1942 to persuade Admiral King to embrace the principles of convoy protection. King was also under pressure from the American Merchant Navy men who were refusing to leave harbour without an escort.

By November 1942, Admiral King began making improvements in convoy defence but it was still a good month for the U-boats as Dönitz remained focused on attacking

Allied merchant shipping wherever he could find it and also opening secondary areas of operation such as Brazil and Freetown

When Jimmy Meeks sailed from Oban on the 1st September 1942, Ultra was still in the midst of a blackout and merchant ships were being sunk at a rate faster than the Allies could build them. To compound the problem, the German equivalent of Bletchley Park, xB-Dienst, had made large progress in breaking the Allied convoys cipher No. 3. Decryptions of this cipher were given the name *Frankfurt* by the Germans.

On 13th December 1942, shortly after Jimmy Meeks arrived home in South Shields, Ultra was back in use. The Allies had captured the latest U-boat signal book from U-559 just before it sank, providing Bletchley Park with the missing piece of the puzzle they needed to decipher the transmissions from the new four-cogged machine. Ultra's reintroduction reduced the number of ships sunk in January and February 1943, as the Submarine Tracking Room was able to direct convoys around waiting U-boat wolf packs. However, the constant re-routing of convoys proved to be very problematic and since many of the re-routing instructions were sent in *Frankfurt*, Dönitz simply redeployed his wolf packs accordingly, allowing the U-boats to gain the upper hand once again. Clearly a change in policy was required to compliment the return of Ultra, as it alone was insufficient to win the U-boat war.

A convoy conference, held by the Allies and attended by the now better informed Admiral King in Washington on the 1st March 1943, resolved to close the convoy air-gaps once and for all. This meant redirecting 120 Liberators from bombing activities in Germany, a directive Air Chief Marshall Arthur *Bomber* Harris, accepted with great reluctance. The Allies also resolved to increase the number of Destroyers protecting the convoys. In addition to these material improvements, the Allies also decided to dispense with their policy of redirecting convoys through the massed U-boat forces and opted to use Ultra to locate U-boats and attack them, in other words they would fight the convoys through the wolf packs. These changes proved to be so successful that the course of the U-boat war in the North Atlantic changed irreversibly in the favour of the Allies in just eight dramatic weeks.

Allied ships in convoy were still attacked and sunk but the U-boat losses were unsustainable and Dönitz had little option but to withdraw his boats to the Black Pit south of the Azores. The Allies renewed their Bay (of Biscay) aerial offensive with a new centrimetric radar resulting in Dönitz's fleet of ten 'milch cow' fuel tankers being sunk following the revelation of their location using Ultra. The Allies had been unaware of the existence of tankers when Ultra was out of commission in 1942, this included U-460, the tanker that supplied U-109 with fuel shortly after it torpedoed the *Peterton*. U-460 was later sunk by US aircraft on the 4th October 1943. Sixty-two men were lost. The loss of their tankers only added to the woes of the beleaguered U-boat fleet and by the end of the year Dönitz had lost 237 U-boats, compared to only 96 in the previous twelve months. By the end of 1943, the U-boat war was effectively over.

This reversal in the fortunes in U-boat power was partly attributable to the skills of one man: Sir Max Horton was appointed Commander of the Western Approaches in

November 1942 by Winston Churchill, who entrusted the Battle of the Atlantic to him. Like Dönitz, Horton was a distinguished submarine captain of World War One and Dönitz considered him a formidable opponent. Under his leadership, the British anti-submarine forces made great improvements in material and technical aspects, but particularly in tactical leadership and morale.

Ultra remained on stream until the end of the war and was kept as a classified secret until 1974. When Karl Dönitz, the U-boat Head of Command, was informed of the secret of Ultra, he exclaimed: 'Ach Doch' (So that's it!). Even after the war, he had completely dismissed the idea that Enigma transmissions were being deciphered; despite knowing the British were monitoring German U-boat movements. He had considered the possibility that the British may have developed some kind of super radar or were simply coordinating sightings and radio traffic in a highly effective manner and believed that treachery was probably the real cause behind their loss of secrecy. He honourably declined the opportunity to update his memoirs, published in 1958, to reflect this revelation.

When he received his Oak Leaves to the Knight's cross a few days after the sinking of the *Peterton*, Bleichrodt was concerned. He admitted to Otto Kohler, former commander of U-377 that he feared for Germany's future. The *Happy Times*, as the U-boat commanders called the successful period in 1940, were over. The most fruitful month for the U-boat fleet in 1942 was November, with an average of 220 tons of Allied shipping sunk each day for every U-boat. However, when this is compared to the tonnage sunk in October 1940, where the figure was 920 tons, it is apparent that the Allies were making life harder for the U-boat fleet even without Ultra.

U-109 Commander Heinrich Bleichrodt's active war ended shortly after the sinking of the *Peterton*. His nerves shredded by repeated depth charging, he eventually succumbed to a nervous breakdown on 26th December 1942 on his seventh tour as commander of U-109. He returned to base on the 23rd January 1943 and was fortunate that his previously good record persuaded Dönitz not to put him in front of a firing squad for dereliction of duty; instead his experience was put to practical use. After five months in the 27th U-boat flotilla, starting in July 1943, Bleichrodt served one year in the 2nd ULD (U-boat training division) as tactical instructor for the officers. On the 1st November 1943 he was promoted to Korvettenkapitän. From July 1944 to the end of the war he was Chief of the 22nd U-boat flotilla.

On his return to Lorient in October 1942, Wolfgang Hirschfeld was forced to visit the Flotilla Surgeon as the fungal disease that had been infecting his skin for some time had become quite serious during U-109's sixth patrol. He was subsequently certified unfit for U-boat duty. Bleichrodt was unhappy that his trusted and experienced radio operator was unable to rejoin U-109 when it sailed on its seventh mission. Hirschfeld shared Bleichrodt's disappointment, lamenting the fact that his friends on U-109 had left without him. Later, he was transferred to the outpatient list and then assigned to the Cipher Room at Kernervel, Lorient, while waiting for another U-boat to join. As it turned out, leaving the doomed U-109 was a good move, but by no means ensured he would survive the war. On the 2nd December 1942, Commander Herbert Schneider brought his boat (U-522) back from its first patrol. It had gone unusually well for them, with 57,000 tons of shipping sunk. Schneider wasn't happy though; he needed an experienced radio operator to train his inexperienced telegraphers. Hirschfeld fitted the bill perfectly and Schneider approached him at the 1942 Christmas celebrations in the U-boat barracks to make him an offer. Although drunk, Hirschfeld wisely asked for 24 hours to consider the offer. Kuddel Wenzel, one of U-109's boatswains on their first mission, was also at the party. He was now Coxswain of U-522. He warned:

'This boat hasn't got very much more time. The skipper does things that make your hair stand on end, like taking bow shots at approaching destroyers.'

Weddel convinced Hirschfeld that U-522 was a U-boat that should be avoided at all costs, and when Schneider returned looking for an answer, Hirschfeld politely demurred. Hirschfeld was destined to become involved in something far more interesting than attacking destroyers head on.

U-522 fulfilled Wenzel's grim prophecy when it sank south-west of Madeira on the 23rd February, blown apart by depth charges fired from British Coastguard Cutter *HMS Totland*. All hands, including Kuddel Wenzel and the maverick Commander, Herbert Schneider, were lost.

Following successful completion of platoon commander training and a warrant officers course in 1943, Hirschfeld joined U-234 on the 20th January 1944. A year later, U-234 was famously ordered to Tokyo with a secret cargo of uranium oxide, mercury, a Me262 jet fighter, engineering blueprints, optical glass and other secret documents. Hitler's intention was to pass on German technology to the Japanese so they could continue the war effort in the likely event of German defeat. The end of hostilities intervened and the commander of U-234 surrendered and sailed into Bergen, Norway. Wolfgang Hirschfeld had survived the war.

U-109 was eventually sunk on the 4th May 1943 south of Ireland (47.22N 22.40W) by a British *Liberator* aircraft (Sqdn. 86/P) flown by Pilot Officer J. C. Green. The U-boat was commanded by Lieutenant Joachim Schramm who had taken over from Bleichrodt on the 1st March 1943. The *Liberator* was on an outbound patrol to link up with convoy HX236 northeast of the Azores when it picked up a contact with its 10cm radar. Shortly afterwards, the crew saw a surfaced U-boat and dropped four depth charges. U-109 began to move in tight circles at about 5 knots, its rudder seemingly damaged by the explosions. Over the next 20 minutes U-109 trailed oil and then slowed to a stop with its stern awash. Although fully surfaced the whole time, none of the crew managed to escape, its hatches probably buckled by the blasts. U-109 sank stern first, at 15:00 hours, the entombed crew plunging to a terrifying and unimaginable death. All fifty-two members of its crew perished. Fourteen of them were teenage boys. Eduard Maureschat, the man who bravely came to the rescue of the *Tuscan Star*'s drowning radio operator, was not onboard at the time. He went on to survive the war. During its 9-patrol career U-109 had sunk a total of thirteen ships (86,501 tons).

Bleichrodt's nervous breakdown and his subsequent transfer to land- based duties saved his life and the lives of five of his officers (including the man who saved them all – Otto Peters) since they were transferred to other boats when U-109 was, temporarily, without a commander.

Ironically, Hirschfeld's embarrassing skin condition saved his skin, since it resulted in his transfer to U-234. He spent the final weeks of the war as a prisoner of war before being released and returning to Germany. Wolfgang Hirschfeld died on the 24th April 2005, aged 88.

At the end of hostilities, Bleichrodt was singled out by the British and accused of war crimes. Many would argue that all U-boat commanders were war criminals, as the indiscriminate nature of their work often resulted in the deaths of youngsters like Teddy Hyde. One also has to question the logic of allowing schoolboys to go to war in the first place. The Merchant Navy may have been a non-combative organisation on paper but the mortality rates for merchant seamen were comparable with many other branches of the armed forces.

The compassion shown by Bleichrodt to Jimmy Meeks and the crew of the *Peterton* in their lifeboats, and the treatment received by Captain Thomas Marrie and the U-109's other captives, Radio Operator Gordon Gill and Captain Caird, suggest that Bleichrodt was certainly not a man who knowingly committed atrocities such as the sinking of the evacuee ship *City of Benares,* which he sank as commander of U-48. In the opinion of the British, Bleichrodt was fully aware of *City of Benares*' human cargo and as a result they wanted him hanged. Bleichrodt was eventually acquitted as he refused to give evidence and no reliable witnesses or documentary proof could be found.

So, did Bleichrodt knowingly murder those civilians? Rolf Hisle (82), a radio operator on the attacking U-boat, U-48, commanded by Heinrich Bleichrodt, may have the answer. In an article published in the International Express (Australia) on the 10th February 2004 entitled: *Reminiscing With The Enemy*, a report of a meeting between himself and Beth Williams, one of only twenty children to survive the sinking of the *City of Benares*, he revealed:

'It was 18 months before the U-48's captain, Heinrich Bleichrodt, discovered the Benares had been carrying children. By that time he had been transferred to another sub (U-109). I took a message to the captain and he was shocked. He said, "Those poor children". The deaths of the children played on his mind terribly and he was weakened by the pounding we had received in the submarines. He was a decent man who had worked his way up to the top. When no one was around, I called him by his first name. He was an officer and a gentleman who never had any time for the Nazis.'

The shattering realisation that he was behind the death of all those children seems to have triggered Bleichrodt's neurosis. His behaviour became increasingly erratic and became especially afraid of Q-ships (anti-submarine warships disguised as merchantmen). The constant depth charging further eroded his resolve and, shortly after sinking the *Peterton*, one of the most decorated commanders in the German U-boat Arm succumbed to a nervous breakdown. After the war Bleichrodt settled into civilian life as the Director of an ironware factory. He died in Munich on the 9th January 1977.

With 27 ships sunk, totalling almost 159,000 tons, Heinrich Bleichrodt ended the war as the tenth most 'successful' U-boat commander out of a total of 1,411 U-boat commanders that saw service in the German U-boat Arm.

The Allies lost a total of 2,828 ships totalling 14.6 millions tons. The vast majority of Allied vessels sunk by U-boats were victims of a surprisingly small percentage of commanders. Some U-boat aces sank up to 47 ships, but the majority of U-boat commanders failed to sink a single ship. Commanders who started out earlier in the war were able to take advantage of much softer targets and were able to perfect their skills. Commanders who entered the war later had to learn their skills in a much more competitive arena. Of the 830 U-boats that saw active service, 696 (84%) were lost to Allied attack.

9

THE WAR GOES ON: 1943 – 1945

By the 19th January 1943, Jimmy Meeks' home leave was over. It seems callous to expect someone so young to return to war so soon after suffering such hardships but the Ministry of War Transport understood the necessity for a quick turnaround of survivors in order to maintain the necessary levels of manning and experience in the Merchant Navy. Jimmy Meeks was no exception to this rule. Manning levels were at such an all time low in 1943 that some ships could not sail simply because they had insufficient crew. Most of Jimmy's shipmates suffered similar treatment, even though some of the men were left mentally and physically scarred by their ordeal. Some, like Mess Boy, Reginald Harrison and Fireman, Samuel Osborne received temporary disability allowances for the 'effects of exposure' but not for long. They were soon declared fit for duty. George Pennington suffered more than most in the aftermath of his 49 day lifeboat voyage. Despite suffering from a severe neurosis brought on by his lifeboat ordeal, he soldiered on until the end of the war and only after hostilities ended in 1945 did he finally request permanent sick leave from the Merchant Navy.

Jack Morley suffered a few sleepless nights in the initial weeks after his ordeal but after two relaxing weeks at Limpsfield Convalescent Home, he was ready for action again and joined a trawler, *The Star of Peace*, and spent a couple of weeks fishing in the Irish Sea.

His close friend, Chas Smith went back to sea but, sadly,

did not survive the war. Working onboard the coastal vessel, *SS Newlands* in April 1945, he was tragically killed when it was sunk by a torpedo off the south east coast of England. He was only 22-years-old.

Veteran Bosun Jimmy Watt carried on sailing, happily for him he was never torpedoed again.

Jolly boat survivor Jimmy Stephenson went back to work too and enjoyed a long career in the Merchant Navy, retiring in the early Eighties. Following his lifeboat voyage he added an extra tattoo to his collection: *In God We Trust'*

Irishman John Ennis was not perturbed by his lifeboat ordeal and he too continued to serve in the Merchant Navy. He would sail on into the post war years and eventually retire from the Merchant Navy in the 1970s.

Cabin boy Dennis Thirkettle continued to serve in the Merchant Navy until the end of the war but his ability to repeatedly annoy his employers would result in the permanent termination of his services at the end of hostilities in 1945.

According to documents maintained in the National Archives, Jimmy Meeks joined a ship called *SS Generton* at the beginning of 1943. Whilst waiting for a researcher at the National Archives to locate and send further details about the movements of this ship, I made contact with the Tyne & Wear Archive in Newcastle, where R. Chapman & Son's voyage ledgers are kept; on the off chance they might contain something interesting. Not for the first time, what looked like a dead end produced some interesting results. In the Voyage Ledger for the *Generton*, which is essentially a book on costs, wages, cargos etc. it was revealed that Jimmy Meeks had been underpaid for the 163-day period (voyage No 17) he was assigned to the *Generton*, from the 2nd January 1943 to 13th

June 1943, by the sum of ten shillings. In times of such hardship Jimmy would not have been pleased about that. It is ironic that this error by his employers would help me to confirm that Jimmy did indeed return to sea as early as 19th January 1943 and that he served on the *Generton* during that time. I was certain that the records I was awaiting from the National Archives would confirm this but the information from the Tyne & Wear Archive opened up an exciting new area of research. *SS Generton* had seen some serious action in March 1943 whilst sailing in convoy OS44 to Gibraltar. The ill-fated convoy was victim to a devastating attack from the German U-boat, U-107, the most successful U-boat in the German Kriegsmarine, operating in wolf pack Robbe and commanded by U-boat ace Harald Gelhaus. Linking Jimmy with those dramatic events showed that his war had not started and ended with the dramatic sinking of the *Peterton* and the subsequent 49 day lifeboat voyage.

Shortly after speaking to Jack Morley for the first time in 2004, I sent him copies of my research on Jimmy Meeks' wartime ship assignments. He called me back a few weeks later with the remarkable news that he, too, had sailed in convoy OS44. He had been onboard *SS Bactria*, bound for the coast of Africa to pick up a cargo of peanuts. A lucky coincidence since he could provide an eyewitness account of U-107's attack on convoy OS44. The attack on convoy OS44 referred to in this chapter is also described from the perspective of the U-boat. Commander Harald Gelhaus' U-boat diary (KTB) for U-107 provides a timeline for the events.

The package of documents obtained from the National Archives provided evidence that Jimmy Meeks may have served on a ship called *SS Generton* during the war. I started looking for information and a photograph of this ship but soon learned that obtaining images of ships that survived the war are far more difficult to find than those that were lost. After a long struggle, I eventually located a photograph of the *Generton* in a library in Sydney, Australia. Following some swift correspondence by e-mail, a photo of the *Generton* was subsequently making a journey that would have taken the ship a month to complete by sea.

Jimmy Meeks said his farewells on the 19th January 1943 and made the short trek to join his new ship, *SS Generton*, in South Shields. The *Generton* (4,781 GRT, 426.5 x 54.0 x 29.0 feet) was a modern vessel compared to the *Peterton*, built in 1936 by long time partners, Short Bros of Sunderland. Keen to improve the efficiency and economy of their ships in the depressed 1930's, Chapman's had opted for a radical new design from German naval architects Misinform G.m.b.H. The main difference compared to standard vessels of the period was the fore-body design, with triangular rather than the more usual 'U' shaped sections and a heavily raked stem. The German designers claimed that the hull form would result in a 2-2$\frac{1}{2}$% increase in cubic capacity, increased stability, wider deck at the forecastle and at least $\frac{1}{2}$ knot increase in service speed, against a penalty of $\frac{1}{4}$% increase in steel weight. Chapman's also opted to build Hermiston and Scorton in the Maierform class. These vessels did not quite live up to expectations. Captain J. A. Simpson, who commanded *Generton* during the war, reported that it was 'difficult to keep up with convoys' but 'its high buoyancy forward did at least give us stability in calm seas'. Captain Terrot Glover Jnr. of the Scorton put the prominent Maeirform bow to good use when he rammed an unidentified U-boat while sailing in convoy

SC121 on the 23rd March 1943. This action earned him the British Empire Medal and 3rd Officer Nicholson a Commendation. Despite their inherent flaws, the three Maierform vessels all completed over 20 years service for Chapman's fleet before they were eventually sold.

SS *Generton*'s crew, like that of the *Peterton*, was dominated by men from South Shields and Hull. The master for the voyage was Captain Elsdon of South Shields. SS *Generton* left the Tyne on the 30th January 1943 and, following a brief stop in Methil, made its way to Hull to await the next convoy to Gibraltar, from where it would proceed to Bone in Algeria with its cargo of coal. Its initial departure was delayed by bad weather. The *Generton* finally left the Clyde on the 6th March 1943 and joined convoy OS44. It was Jimmy Meeks' second foreign bound voyage and only days after the Allies had finally agreed to close the air gaps. If he thought that he had already met his first and last U-boat of World War Two, then he was mistaken. The attack on convoy OS44 is one of the most savage recorded by any single U-boat in World War Two.

The final destination of convoy OS44 (code word *Mangle*) was Freetown. This meant that the *Generton* would leave the convoy earlier than anticipated and sail through the straits of Gibraltar together with other Mediterranean-bound vessels (*Oporto, Ronan, Gudrun Mærsk* and *Empire Sunbeam*).

Ships operated by R. Chapman and Son were frequent members of the OS series of convoys. The OS series of convoys catered for vessels entering the South Atlantic and carried vessels from UK ports to the collection point off Freetown in Sierra Leone. Vessels sailing to South America or onward to the Cape would be detached from the convoy at suitable points. Prior to OS52/KMS21 (when the Mediterranean was opened) the OS series also included vessels sailing to India which subsequently sailed in the KMS section. Although the complementary SL convoy series, from Freetown to the UK, had been sailing since September 1939, the OS series only began in July 1941, by which time some forty SL convoys had been escorted. The OS series continued until September 1942 (OS42) when it was suspended for five months to free resources for *Operation Torch*, the invasion of North Africa, which began on the 8th November 1942. The series recommenced in February 1943 and in April 1943 was combined with the KMS series bound for Gibraltar with the two convoys separating en route. The OS series continued until May 1945 (OS131/KMS105). Data for every convoy that sailed in the Second World War is available from original sources contained in the National Archives. Information can also be obtained from *The Allied Convoy System 1939-1945* by Arthur Hague. The National Archive data records the homeport, destination, cargo, nationality, armament and pendant number (position in a convoy) for each vessel in convoy. Vessels that had intended to travel in convoy but had not sailed are also noted in the archive's records. Vessels that did not sail usually found the preceding or subsequent convoy or, as in the case of the *Peterton*, a convoy that would take them at least part of the way.

Jimmy Meeks and the *Generton* were allocated pendant number 65 in convoy OS44. This placed it in the sixth column and the fifth and last row at the rear of the convoy. Convoy OS44 left Liverpool on the 6th March 1943 with 46 ships. The *City of Leicester* (74) and the *Bosworth* (75) occupied spaces on the *Generton*'s starboard beam but returned to port shortly afterwards, mechanical problems being the most likely cause. The *Oporto* (84) and the *Clan Alpine* (85) then became the *Generton*'s nearest neighbours to starboard. Directly in front of the *Generton*, was the British vessel *SS Marcella* (64) and in front of it was the Dutch vessel, *SS Djambi* (63). Elsewhere in the convoy, were two more Chapman vessels; the *Amberton* (112) and the *Uranienborg* (43). The convoy would split once they reached Gibraltar, with the *Generton* and the other Mediterranean-bound ships heading through the Straits of Gibraltar and the rest continuing down to Freetown, which they planned to reach by the 24th March 1943. The convoy was escorted by Group 39 Ocean Escort which included: *HMS Rochester, HMS Scarborough, HMS Fleetwood, HMS Coltsfoot, HMS Spirra, HMS Mignonette, HMS Blasam, HMS Asalxa* and *HMS Cowslip*.

Able Seaman Jack Morley was onboard the *Bactria* (pendant 24) bound for the African coast where it was to pick up a cargo of peanuts.

On the 30th January 1943, Commander Harald Gelhaus (Knights Cross) guided U-107 out of its base in Lorient. U-107 is a type IXB boat of the same design as U-109. It had been laid down at the same AG Weser yard in Bremen on the 6th December 1939 and was part of the 2nd U-boat flotilla. Under its first commander, Karl Dönitz's son-in-law, Commander Günter Hessler (Knights Cross), U-107 had already racked up a long list of Allied victims, including 14 vessels in a single patrol, carried out in an area of operations between the Canary Islands and Freetown, in the spring of 1941. Commander Harald Gelhaus took over command of U-107 on the 1st December 1941. He began his naval career in April

1935, serving on the light cruiser, *Karlsruhe*, and on the battleship *Gneisenau*. In October 1939 he transferred to the U-boat force where his first three patrols were as IWO on U-103 under Commander Schütze. He left the boat in March 1941 and took command of U-143 a type IIB boat. After four patrols he became the commander of U-107. By the 30th January 1943, he had become a seasoned and much respected U-boat commander.

As U-107 entered the Bay of Biscay, it ran into a storm. Large waves breaking over its conning tower caused water to cascade through its hatches and subsequently led to a small fire in an auxiliary switchboard. However, it was quickly extinguished and U-107 was soon able to continue with its mission.

On the 3rd February 1943, Gelhaus received orders from BdU to join Feiler, von Manstein, Huttemann, Schafer and Eppen in grid square BE 6723 (Bay of Biscay). U-107 then spent the next few days repeatedly diving to avoid approaching Allied reconnaissance planes. On the 11th February they received fresh orders from BdU to join the *Dolphin* wolf pack in grid square CG 4515 (west coast of Spain). *Dolphin* was established for the purpose of attacking new tanker convoys from Port of Spain or the Mediterranean in Operation Torch. U-107 continued to be thwarted by Allied reconnaissance aircraft and Gelhaus was becoming increasingly frustrated at his lack of progress:

> *Commander:* As soon as I surface and forge on, I am again spotted and must go down again. Due to the many alarms and avoidance manoeuvres it was not possible to put the air pumps on and my air came

down to 90 cubic metres.

On the 16th February 1943, U-107 was dispatched to wolf pack *Robbe*. Six days later it sighted motor freighter *SS Roxborough Castle* (7,801 BRT) sailing unescorted on its way to Buenos Aires with 1,030 tons of chemical products and post:

> 22.02.43
> CE 6612   03:09
> Steamer – Shadow ➜ SW in sight. Approach.
> CE 6834   08:23
> A-↓ for an underwater attack
> Steamer sinks lower in the water but does not sink.
> Lifeboats launched in the water.
> CE 6837   09:12
> Fan shot, Tube VI – Hit Engine Room
> Steamer lies on to its side, sinks. Surface, and the (life) boats driven near – questioning.
> The captain is not arrested, there is no room for him.

One of the sixty-four survivors (no casualties) was Gus Britton. He reported the contact of *Roxborough Castle's* lifeboats with Commander Gelhaus and U-107:

> 'The same officer whom we thought to be the captain asked us (in perfect English): "did we have any injured, did we need any food and water, did we specially need anything at all?" We thanked him and answered "No" to his questions. He then apologised for sinking us and told us how far it was to St Miguel,

gave us a course to steer by and wished us good luck and left.'

U-107 spent the next few days diving repeatedly to avoid Allied reconnaissance planes and destroyers. It also ran into some steamers, but, on both occasions, the vessels were identified as neutral and left alone. Then on the 2nd March 1943, U-511 reported the sighting of *SS Generton*'s convoy (OS44). Allied aircraft continued to harass U-107 and two depth charges from a flying boat caused what initially seemed to be just minor damage but, two days later, heavier damage was discovered on the locking mechanism of one of their torpedo tubes.

On the 5th March 1943, Gelhaus received a fresh update on the convoy location from U-445 and finally sighted convoy OS44 the following morning:

(KTB Note: ↑ U-boat surfaces, ↓ U-boat dives)
06.03.43   CG 8161
08:00 underwater – several detonations heard.
08:10 ↑ Numerous masts and 2 DE (*Destroyers*) in sight

Heavy aircraft reconnaissance again forced U-107 down where it was unable to move and lost contact with the convoy later in the afternoon. It picked up the convoy again on the 9th March 1943 only to lose them for a second time when another reconnaissance plane forced it to dive.

On the 12th March 1943 Gelhaus received an update on the progress of convoy OS44 from BdU and set the required course to intercept:

12.03.43   CG 1493
17:15 *BdU FT:* Radio announcement 13:00 hrs Convoy (*OS44*) in BE 9284
Commander: I am positioned favourably and call in my GF reply

The masters, officers and crew of most of the ships in convoy OS44 were well aware they were being shadowed by wolf pack *Robbe*. Repeated reports of U-boat sightings in the area (including U-107) and Ultra decryptions of BdU's radio traffic saw to that. Knowledge of this kind served to increase the vigilance of the crew, quite possibly sending their tension levels soaring too.

Prior to sailing, it was agreed that the convoy's columns should be separated by a distance of 5 cables (1,000 yards) but the Commodore might have reduced this to 3 cables (600 yards), something they had planned to do anyway once they had crossed latitude 7° West, in order to reduce the chances of U-boat infiltration and to make the escorts' job easier. With a cruising speed of only 8 knots, they were not in any position to outrun their pursuers.

By 05:00 hours on the morning of the 13th March 1943, U-107 had convoy OS44 in her sights:

13.03.43   CG 1139
05:10 Shadows, Destroyers and Steamers in sight.
05:30 Wind up the approach. Tubes I-VI fired at the steamers. After the shots, turned off – hedge run
During the rotation (*Gelhaus was turning his boat round so he could fire his two aft torpedoes*) four detonations are detected.

SS *Oporto* (2,352 BRT) sailing on the *Generton*'s starboard beam was hit by one of the torpedoes. It had been carrying a cargo of 1,500 tons of copper sulphate, 413 tons of seed potatoes and mail from Liverpool to Seville and sank in position 42.45N 13.31W, (190 miles west of Cape Finisterre). *HMS Spiraea* picked up only four survivors, who were transferred to *HMS Gentian* (K90) before being landed in Gibraltar. The Master and thirty-six crewmembers are commemorated on Tower Hill panel 76. Five of the ship's gunners remain unidentified.

Also struck was *SS Sembilangan* (4,990 BRT), located in the ninth column of the convoy. The torpedo ignited its cargo of ammunition and all but one of the crew was killed in the ensuing explosions. The crew on the *Djambi* later reported that the *Sembilangan* 'flew into the sky' and agreed that 'no-one could have survived that catastrophe'. The master, P. M. Leguit, and a total of eighty-five crewmembers were lost. The single survivor was the 4th Engineer, who had been thrown overboard by the explosion.

SS Clan Alpine (7,374 BRT), captained by Joseph Henry Crellin, was the third vessel to be struck by one of the six torpedoes fired from U-107. It did not sink immediately but, being dead in the water, was later scuttled with two depth charges dropped by *HMS Scarborough*. There were 26 dead and 69 survivors.

SS Generton's crew were rattled and some started running to the lifeboats.

> *Captain Elsdon:* At 5:15 M. Bentley, 3rd Eng, fell down on deck during a scrimmage for the lifeboats, due to enemy action and hurt his right knee.

Jack Baron on Generton: We weren't ordered to the lifeboats but some of the crew sometimes did try to get into them when we were under attack.

Three ships sunk from a spread of six torpedoes represented a good return for U-107 but its eager commander had unfinished business. Seven minutes later he turned his boat around and was ready for a new attack, this time firing from his aft torpedo tubes:

13.03.43   CG 1218
05:37 Shots from tubes V and VI – hit was a terrible one, enormous detonation, a glowing red cloud ascends. The steamer flies into air.

The unfortunate vessel was *SS Marcella* (4,592 BRT). It had been carrying 6,800 tons of ammunition to Table Bay, Cape Town, South Africa. Not surprisingly, the explosion wiped out its entire compliment of 44 men. *Marcella*, with pendant number 64, had been sailing directly in front of the *Generton*. The distance between ships in the convoy columns had been reduced to 3 cables (approx. 600 yards), so the catastrophic loss of the *Marcella* was witnessed in all its graphic detail by the *Generton*'s crew and left them reeling. One of the *Marcella*'s victims was 17-year-old cabin boy Gordon Singleton; it was only his second voyage.

J. A. Morley on Bactria: We didn't sleep at all that night. The explosion when *Marcella* went up was enormous. During the war I saw a lot of tankers go up in flames and seeing men struggling in the water, that was the worst, it was mind-boggling.

Jack Baron on Generton: Jimmy Meeks and I had just completed our watch together when the first torpedoes hit. By that stage of the war we slept in our clothes and lifejacket so we were able to quickly get up and man our battle stations. Out on the deck I saw the fireworks as the ship ahead of us (*Marcella*) was hit, she went up in the air and when she came down there was nothing left of her.

The *Generton* sailed bravely onwards. Captain C. A. W. van Dijk of the Dutch owned *SS Djambi*, sailing directly in front of the *Marcella* and now with the *Generton* in its wake, was so shaken by the bombardment he detached from the convoy. He did this without authorization from the Commodore, an action that would have deadly consequences for his ship and the Vice Commodore's vessel, *SS Silverbeech*.

Captain Van Dijk was concerned for the safety of his vessel; the losses of the *Marcella, Oporto, Sembilangan* and *Clan McAlpine* had left him unnerved. He was no novice, having sailed in many convoys, but the constant tension and severity of U-107's attack finally broke his resolve. *Djambi's* Quartermaster, J. Rose, later reported that Van Dijk turned to him and said 'I'm off!'

The convoy's Commodore, F. A. Marten, on the *Sansu*, gave the signal for all ships to return fire on the U-boat. However, the dim early morning light was not sufficient to allow more than a few sporadic shots to be aimed at the U-boat. At the same time he ordered the *Generton* to fill the gap left by the *Marcella* and *Djambi* and hold station behind the Belgian vessel *Copa Cobana*.

Harald Gelhaus and U-107 decided to lie low for a while. Daylight was approaching and the inevitable depth charge attack from the convoy escorts would soon start. Although Gelhaus reported several detonations, nothing came close enough to cause them any concern. U-107 surfaced again at 13:00 hours. By then the convoy was out of sight and they found themselves slowly steaming through a huge field of wreckage that they had created.

After steering a zigzag course for 2 hours, Van Dijk decided to return the *Djambi* to its convoy position. This would be difficult due to the fact that the vessels around the *Djambi's* convoy station had closed up to fill the gaps. SS *Generton*, in particular, had some motoring to do as it was completely isolated by the losses. The *Djambi's* master then miscalculated the distance to the Vice Commodore's ship, SS *Silverbeech* (81). The *Silverbeech*, in turn, was unable to read the intentions of the rapidly approaching *Djambi* and at 07:05 hours on the 13th March 1943; the *Djambi* struck the *Silverbeech* and opened up a huge gash in its own hull. After the collision, the ships turned parallel to each other and the *Silverbeech* slid to the back. The *Djambi* began to sink almost immediately and Captain Van Dijk gave the order to abandon ship. The lifeboats were launched and within a few minutes the crew were safely onboard the boats and able to watch the *Djambi* slide beneath the waves. Barely 16 minutes had passed since the initial collision. The British frigate, *HMS Fleetwood*, sailing alongside, quickly picked up the survivors ensuring there were no victims.

Having shaken off the convoy escorts, Gelhaus and U-107

set off again in search of OS44. Not for the first time, they were forced to dive by Allied reconnaissance planes but at 11:41 hours on the 14th March 1943, its lookouts relocated the convoy:

14.03.43   CG 18
00:06 – 04:00 3x A-↓ reconnaissance plane
14.03.43   CG 4634
11:41 Convoy again in view

Before they could launch a new attack, an Allied flying boat arrived and forced U-107 to submerge again. When they resurfaced, Gelhaus was soon forced to dive again as Allied reconnaissance planes circled overhead. Realising the convoy's air protection was now too good, Gelhaus finally gave up and retreated:

> *Commander:* I halt convoy operations in these areas; the Englishmen have such heavy air surveillance, that it is not promising. One can only stand still and hope by coincidence a vessel comes along.

On the 16th March 1943, U-107 came across two empty lifeboats. One of them was a *Clan Alpine* boat and the other from the *Baharistan*. The latter vessel must have lowered a boat to assist survivors from *Clan Alpine* because the *Baharistan* was not one of the convoy victims, in fact it would go on to survive the war.

Back in Grid Square BE 6137, U-107 received a radio signal from U-621; they had spotted a new convoy. Gelhaus plotted a course to intercept but was forced to give up as his fuel reserves were running low. He plotted a course for home; it had been a very successful patrol.

The survivors from the *Djambi* were transferred from *HMS Fleetwood* onto the *Generton* where Jimmy Meeks, Jack Baron and the rest of the crew tended to their needs until they were dropped off in Gibraltar. Once in Gibraltar, the *Djambi* crewmen did not have to wait very long for a UK-bound vessel to take them home.

The Vice Commodore's ship, *SS Silverbeech*, was so badly damaged by the collision with the *Djambi* that it had to leave the convoy and seek repairs. It is believed that it made for Gibraltar since it later hooked up with convoy RS3 (Gibraltar – Freetown) to continue its voyage. However, only 15 days after the collision, on the 28th March 1943, *SS Silverbeech* was torpedoed by U-172. There were 7 survivors and 62 men lost their lives. The position was 25.20N 15.55W, 70 miles off the coast of Western Sahara.

U-107 arrived back in Lorient on the 25th March 1943. Dönitz was satisfied:

> *BdU:* Very well accomplished mission by a proven commander.
>
> A successful demonstration that Gibraltar convoy routes can be attacked is acknowledged. Much is owed to the tenacity, bravery and the tactical knowledge of the commander. Five steamers at 29,801 BRT are confirmed.

Commander Gelhaus closed his report with the telling analysis that his boat had submerged 168 times during the patrol, including 127 times due to enemy alarms. These figures perfectly demonstrated the effectiveness of air cover and the importance of the decision made on the 1st March 1943 to close the remaining air-gaps.

Faced with such formidable levels of convoy protection, successes were clearly unsustainable and, despite Dönitz's assertions that Gibraltar bound convoys could be attacked, OS convoys never again suffered such dramatic losses. SS *Generton*'s 3rd Engineer M. Bennett, injured during the attack, was later hospitalised in Gibraltar where he would remain until the *Generton* picked him up on the return trip.

Although Jimmy Meeks emerged from convoy OS44 physically unscathed, the torment of being shadowed by U-107 and wolf pack *Robbe* for days at a time and then witnessing neighbouring vessels erupt into fiery infernos may have left him and the crew of the *Generton* with some permanent mental scars.

The *Djambi*'s Master, Captain Van Dijk, subsequently faced an inquiry into the collision and the loss of his vessel. He was found to be negligent and directly responsible for the collision but escaped prosecution since his previous record had been good.

Jimmy Meeks' third foreign-going voyage was his first trans-Atlantic voyage of the war and the first one on which he was spared the terror of a U-boat attack. Until then he must have believed that the deck of a ship was the most hazardous place in the world. The *Generton* departed Oban on the 4th July 1943 and joined a convoy bound for Halifax, Nova Scotia in Canada (probably ONS-12). Their voyage was uneventful and they arrived safely on 18th July 1943. That the voyage went without incident does not mean it was stress free. Atlantic convoys had been the targets of U-boats for the duration of the war and although the tide of the war was turning, the North Atlantic still contained a U-boat threat. Jimmy would have to run the gauntlet of trans-Atlantic crossings seven more times before the war was over.

Return voyages normally sailed in either an HX or SC convoy. The HX series of convoys (1939–1945), between Halifax, Nova Scotia and Liverpool, was the longest continuous Atlantic convoy series of the war. The first convoy, HX1 sailed on 16th September 1939 and the final convoy, HX358, left Halifax on the 23rd May 1945. The speed was set initially at 9 knots, which excluded many older ships. These were forced to sail alone with disastrous results. The HX series lost only 96 ships to U-boats, of which 60 were stragglers. The success of this series of convoys is indisputable.

The SC convoy series was introduced in 1940 to cater for slower vessels that struggled to maintain the 9-knot minimum. The initial speed here was set at $7^{1}/_{2}$ knots. To avoid congestion with the HX convoy, the SC series used Sydney, Cape Breton, as its western terminal.

The first SC convoy, SC1, sailed on the 15th August 1940 and the last, SC177, left Sydney, Cape Breton on the 8th August 1945. 143 vessels were lost to U-boats in this period. Clearly the SC convoys were more susceptible than their HX equivalent to U-boat losses. The slower SC convoys suffered from a reduced ability to divert around awaiting U-boats (twice as many SC convoys were detected as HX convoys) and the older vessels were less able to cope once an attack occurred. Not surprisingly, merchant seamen loathed the SC series.

The *Generton*'s return voyage to Loch Ewe, Scotland, on the 10th August 1943 most likely occurred in one of the unpopular SC convoys, SC139. Although still summer, the weather was causing problems, a harsh reminder that even without U-boats the North Atlantic was still an extremely hazardous place for a ship. Convoy Commodore:

'The convoy (HX251) worked its way unusually slowly forwards due to the strong headwinds and high seas. The poor weather and rough seas made it necessary for several ships to stop and secure their loads and to make repairs.

'We had a strong north-easterly storm one day and strong headwinds for three days.'

No other ships were lost and the *Generton* made it safely back to Loch Ewe with its cargo of wood pulp.

Only a handful of ships were sunk by U-boats in the North Atlantic in the month of August 1943. U-107, now commanded by Volker Simmermacher, sank the US vessel the *Albert Gallatin*. Other than that, successes were few and far between. U-732, commanded by Klaus-Peter Carlsen (no relation to the author), U-185, U-566 and U-757 were the only other U-boats to report any successes.

Jimmy Meeks would make one more trip to Canada onboard the *Generton* in November 1943. That voyage too proved uneventful, a clear sign that the U-boat war was all but over. And he would enjoy the luxury of Christmas at home as the *Generton* was in port in Hull and in need of some essential repairs. The advent of the Christmas holidays might well have persuaded the ship's Master that the repairs were more essential than they truly were.

One of Jimmy Meeks' last voyages onboard the *Generton*

was in convoy OS65/KMS39, which departed Loch Ewe, Scotland on the 14th January 1944. The *Generton* (pendant 52) was loaded with potatoes and vehicles and its final destination this time was Sicily. They would sail together as far as Gibraltar, OS65 would then continue on to Freetown but the *Generton* and the rest of KMS39 would detach and sail together through the Straits of Gibraltar before dispersing to their final destinations. *SS Generton* was joined in the convoy by two other Chapman vessels, the Ministry of War Transport vessel, the *Empire Cormorant*, and the tireless *SS Innerton*, on what was probably its last major voyage before being scuttled in June later that year.

On the 19th January 1944, off the coast of Ireland, 360 miles west of Cape Clear, they were sighted by a *Heinkel 177*. Of the U-boats subsequently directed to the scene, only one, U-641, managed to make contact. Shortly afterwards, *HMS Violet*, located on the outer of the three-ring convoy escort, picked up a signal from U-641. Captain C. N. Stewart then proceeded to demonstrate the search and destroy tactic that had proved to so decisive in the U-boat war. He altered course immediately to intercept, planning to ram the U-boat if he could get close enough. U-641 saw the destroyer coming and crash-dived as *HMS Violet* fired a single round over its submerging conning tower. *HMS Violet's* ASDIC operator quickly picked up a signal from U-641 as it turned away. Captain Stewart decided to launch a hedgehog attack, increasing speed to 8 knots and firing off his first pattern. Three of the twenty-four projectiles were heard to explode. At 19:35 hours an oil patch was observed and a second hedgehog attack was made to finish off what was left of the stricken U-boat. U-641 had been ruthlessly and efficiently despatched by a single destroyer with the loss of all hands. A testament to the advantages held by the Allies in terms of numbers, equipment, tactics and signal intelligence.

SS Generton proved to be a lucky ship for Jimmy Meeks but he would soon be transferring to *SS Grainton*.

The crew of U-107 were not so lucky. U-107 was sunk under the command of Lieutenant Karl-Heinz Fritz on the 18th August 1944, in the Bay of Biscay west of La Rochelle, in position 46.46N, 03.49W, by depth charges from a British Sunderland aircraft (Sqdn. 201/W). All fifty-eight hands were lost. By the time of its loss, U-107 had accounted for an incredible thirty-nine ships (217,786 tons) in a 14-patrol career between the 1st January 1941 and the 18th August 1944.

Commander Harald Gelhaus left U-107 in 1943 to become a staff member of the OKM, the High Command of the German Navy. He had sunk 19 ships, totaling 100,373 tons. In February 1944, he became a training officer in the 22nd and 27th flotillas and spent the final months of the war in various staff positions, the last one being in Naval High Command North. At the end of the war, he spent three months in Allied captivity. Harald Gelhaus died on the 2nd December 1997.

Jimmy Meeks joined *SS Grainton* (6,341 GRT, 423.0 x 58.3 x 29.8 feet) in Gibraltar on the 11th March 1944. It is not clear why he joined this ship. He may have been instructed to do so by his employer (he was still only 18-years old) or perhaps he just felt like a change – after all *Generton* had been through the mangle.

SS Generton sailed unmolested without Jimmy for the remainder of the war and went on into post war service. R.

SS Generton: 4,907 GRT. 427 feet long. Built in 1936 for R. Chapman & Son of Newcastle by Short Bros, Sunderland. Jimmy Meeks joined this vessel on 19th January 1943 and sailed with it until 11th March 1944. *Generton* was fortunate to survive when U-107 hit Convoy OS44 in March 1943 and sank virtually everything around it. *(J. Clarkson – Chapman of Newcastle).*

Chapman & Son sold it off in 1955 to Paulins Rederi AB (Finland) for the princely sum of £235,000 and it was renamed *Imatra*. In 1959 it was bought by the Sun Wah Shipping Company and renamed *Capella*. It was later sold again to Cia Nav. Pearl SA in 1966 and renamed *Bucentaur*. In 1968 it received its fifth and final name, *Bangkok Trader*. The same year it developed leaks whilst on a voyage from Bangkok to Osaka and was towed into a Taiwanese ship breaker at Kaohsiung where a fire sealed its fate and it was broken up. The war was long since forgotten and the *Generton* was just another tramp steamer coming to an ignominious end.

Like many of Chapman's ships, the *Grainton* had seen plenty of service and action during the war. It had been part

U-107: Approaches unidentified lifeboat to interrogate survivors and offer assistance, 1941. Commander Gunther Hessler, son-in-law of Karl Dönitz, commanded U-107 at the time. Jimmy Meeks and his new ship, *SS Generton* and Jack Morley on *SS Bactria* ran into U-107 in March 1943, when it latched onto convoy OS 44. Five ships were sunk but *Generton* and *Bactria* were not amongst them.
(Bundesarchiv)

of convoy OS33 decimated by U-boat wolf pack *Hai* (Shark) where 11 of the convoy's forty-five ships were lost. However, with Jimmy onboard, the *Grainton* became unusually inactive in the first half of 1944, spending a lot of time in ship repair yards as its engine and boilers repeatedly broke down. It was holed up in South Shields for two months from May 1944 undergoing essential repairs, which at least gave Jimmy an unexpected opportunity to rest and recharge his batteries in the comfort of his home town.

Jimmy Meeks made two more trips across the Atlantic during his tenure on the *Grainton* but Dönitz's permanent

SS Grainton (2) renamed as (KATHARINA DOROTHEA FRITZEN): 6,341 GRT. 423 feet long. Photographed in South Africa. Built in 1929 for R. Chapman & Son of Newcastle by Short Bros, Sunderland. Jimmy Meeks joined this vessel on 11th March 1944 and sailed with her until the end of the war and during the immediate post-war years. *(www.blueislandivers.com)*

retreat in the battle for the Atlantic meant that he had seen his last U-boat. On the first of those voyages, the *Grainton* left Greenock, Scotland, on the 2nd August 1944 and joined a westbound convoy (ON247) and two weeks later they entered the vast St Lawrence River and docked in Montreal on the 15th August 1944.

Grainton's Ship Movement Log at the National Archive confirmed its presence in convoy HX306 (fast) for the return journey in September 1944. Later that year, the *Grainton* returned to North America and the St Lawrence River, this time docking in the port of Sorel on 19th November 1944, following another uneventful voyage from Loch Ewe (convoy ONS35 or ON263). The return voyage was made in slow-moving convoy SC163. This convoy left Sydney, Canada on the 17th December 1944, and the crew celebrated Christmas in the North Atlantic. *SS Grainton* would arrive in Loch Ewe on the 31st December 1944, just in time for the New Year celebrations.

Jimmy Meeks was clearly comfortable with the ship and its crew as he continued to sail on the *Grainton* after the war. He eventually left the *Grainton* in 1947 and joined *SS Dumfries* as 3rd Mate.

Buenos Aires was the destination of Jimmy Meeks' first wartime voyage and, as it turned out, the destination of his last. *SS Grainton* left Southend on the 17th March 1945 and, following a short stop in Rosario, Brazil, steamed up the River Plate and docked in Buenos Aires on the 27th April 1945. The irony cannot have escaped Jimmy and he had plenty of time to reflect on his ill-fated first voyage on the *Peterton* during the *Grainton's* five-week voyage into the South Atlantic. *SS Grainton* departed Buenos Aires three days before *VE Day* on the 8th May 1945, so Jimmy and his crewmates celebrated the end of the war in the South Atlantic, miles away from family and friends. Convoys would continue to function for several more months until the Japanese surrender but the war was effectively over and Jimmy Meeks experienced for the first time, the sensation of peacetime sailing, free from the fear and anxiety of the U-boat menace.

CONVOY OS44 CRUISING ORDER

Convoy Speed = 8 knots ←

R. Chapman & Sons

1	2	3 Rear Commodore	4	5 Commodore	6	7	8 Vice Commodore	9	10	11
▲ Baron Tweedmouth 11	▲ Baron Ramsay 21	▲ New Colombia 31	▲ Corabella 41	▲ Sansu 51	▲ Isipingo 61	▲ Marwarri 71	Silverbeech 81 DAMAGED COLLISION	▲ Empire Glade 91	▲ Markhor 101	Tordene 111
▲ Begum 12	▲ Henri Jasper 22	▲ Alphard — DID NOT SAIL	▲ Maradian (T) 42	▲ Deido 52	▲ Copa Cobana (Bel) 62	▲ City of Worcester 72	▲ African Prince 82	Semblangan (NL) 92 SUNK BY U107	▲ Lieut. St. Loubert Bie 102	Amberton 112
Cap Cantin Ø 13	Danae II Ø 22 — DID NOT SAIL	▲ Celtic Star 33	▲ Uranienborg 43	▲ Dordrecht 53	▲ Djambi (NL) 63 SUNK IN COLLISION	▲ Asphalion 73	▲ Menelaus 83	▲ Sembilan (NL) 93	▲ City of Sydney 103	▲ Hoperidge 113
▲ Pendeen 14	Bactria Ø 24	Empire Sunbeam 34	Gudrun Mærsk 44	Ronan 54	▲ Marcella 64 SUNK BY U107	City of Leicester RETURNED TO PORT	▲ Clan Alpine 84 SUNK BY U107	▲ City of Windsor 94	▲ Baharistan 104	▲ Fort Wedderburne 114 (NL)
		Baron Napier 35	Algerian 45	City of Lancaster 55	Generton 65	Bosworth RETURNED TO PORT	Oporto 85 SUNK BY U107			

▲ Ships for Freetown
▲ Ships for Walvis Bay, Cape Town
Ø Ships for Bathurst
● Ships for South America
--- Ships for Portugal and Spain
= Ships for Gibraltar and Med.

Convoy OS44: U-107 sinks four ships in Gibraltar/Freetown-bound convoy OS44 on 13th March 1943. Jimmy Meeks on the *Generton* and former crewmate Jack Morley on the *Bactria* were very fortunate to survive this attack as all of the ships in their immediate vicinity were sunk, in some cases, accompanied by enormous explosions as stores of ammunition ignited. Commander Harald Gelhaus returned U-107 to base when anti-submarine aircraft rendered further attacks impossible.

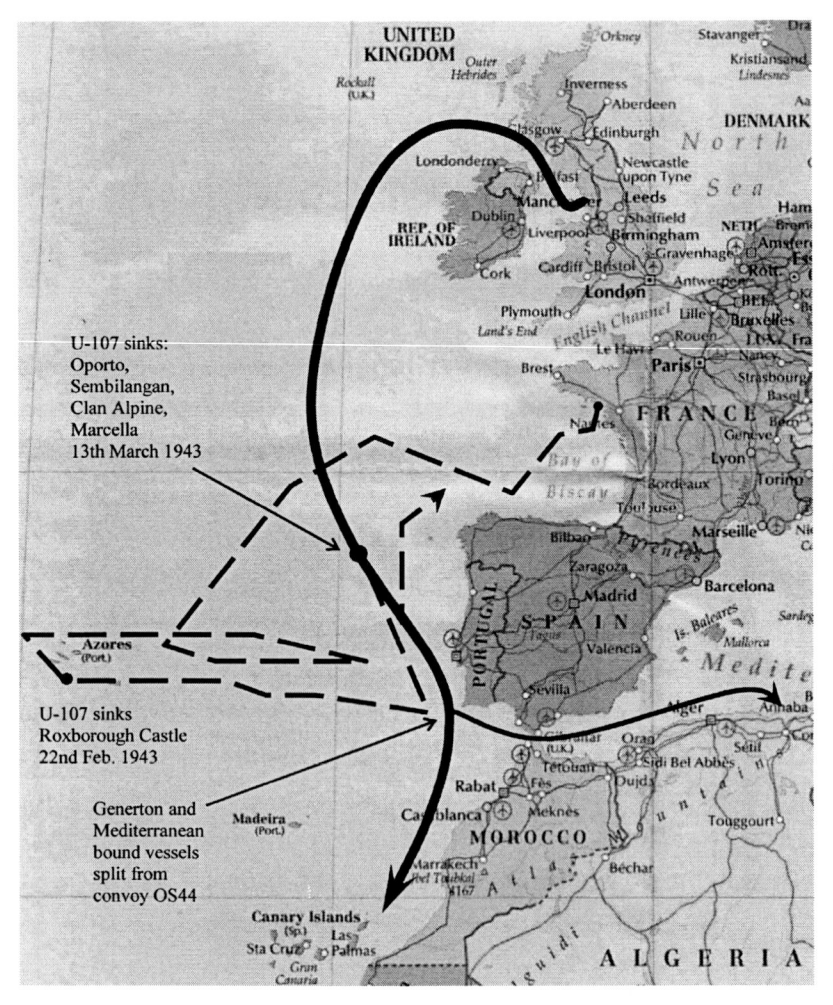

SS Generton ▬▬▬▬▬   Convoy OS44 ▬▬▬▬▬
U-107 Patrol ▬ ▬ ▬ ▬

U-107 sinks:
Oporto,
Sembilangan,
Clan Alpine,
Marcella
13th March 1943

U-107 sinks
Roxborough Castle
22nd Feb. 1943

Generton and
Mediterranean
bound vessels
split from
convoy OS44

10

RETURN TO FREETOWN – THE POST WAR YEARS

Jimmy Meeks made an emotional return to Freetown shortly after the war. The timing of his return is uncertain, but it seems likely it was while serving on Chapman's SS Grainton in 1947.

On their arrival in Freetown, Jimmy Meeks and his crewmates took the opportunity to visit Teddy Hyde's grave in the King Tom Cemetery, only a short distance from the port, located in the northern district of the town, with the intention of paying their respects. They were not at all pleased at the sight that greeted them. Teddy's grave was overgrown and the cross erected in 1942 had gone missing. The men immediately took the curator to task and enlisted the services of a cemetery worker to help clear the grave, plant some fresh flowers and erect a newly inscribed cross. Unable to tend the grave themselves, Jimmy paid a local man to keep up future maintenance. Once everything was settled, the crew photographed the now immaculate plot and took a few moments to pay their respects and reflect on the short life of a friend they had known for weeks but would remember forever.

On his return to England, Jimmy made the short trip from South Shields to Barbara Hyde's home in Cullercoats. According to Teddy's sister, Isabel, Jimmy's thoughtful act was greatly appreciated by their mother:

I clearly remember Barbara (Hyde) telling us about this smart young man who came to see her and brought her the photographs and how very upset he became. It made a great impression on her as you can imagine.

It was a rare show of emotion from a man not normally noted for it. Teddy's death sat deep in Jimmy's conscience. His kind words and the knowledge that her son's grave was in good hands, helped to comfort Barbara Hyde and allow her to come to terms with the loss of her son.

Isabel McGregor: It fades over the years but we celebrated Teddy's birthday every year. If any of us were away from home, we always contacted our mother on 5th, April.

Barbara Hyde coped with her grief in silence and did not talk about her loss to anyone in her family. She kept Jimmy's photographs from Freetown in a bag together with Teddy's last letter. The documents were found by her family on her death in 1988.

The Commonwealth War Graves Commission protects the interests of all international war gravesites. The King Tom Cemetery is now a very well maintained graveyard and since the Commonwealth War Graves Commission has Teddy Hyde's final resting place logged in its register, we can assume that the services of the local caretaker are no longer needed.

Jimmy Meeks (Left) 1947: Looking understandably older than his 20-years, posing with two shipmates in Port Said, March 28th, 1947. Probably taken onboard SS Grainton.
(Janice Levett – Private Collection)

Jimmy Meeks (Left), King Tom Cemetery, Freetown, Sierra Leone (Late 1940's): Edward Hyde's grave had fallen into disrepair. Jimmy Meeks and crewmates tended to the plot and erected a new cross with the words "EDWARD HYDE, Died 14th Nov 1942 (*actual date was 16th Nov 1942*). Following Enemy Action. Remembered by his shipmates. Aged 15 years". *(Isabel McGregor – Private Collection)*

Jimmy Meeks at Edward Hyde's grave, King Tom Cemetery, Freetown (late 1940's): Edward Hyde's grave restored; Jimmy Meeks took a moment to reflect on the short life of his friend.
(Isabel McGregor – Private Collection)

HMS Bronington (late 1970's): Captain HRH Prince Charles (second from right) and Jimmy Meeks (third from left) piloting Prince Charles' first command, HMS Bronington, into Workington harbour. Prince Charles took command of HMS Bronington in 1976.
(Janice Levett – Private Collection).'

Trinity House Pilots for Workington & Whitehaven (1980's): James Nicholson Meeks (second from right).
(Janice Levett – Private Collection)

Isabel McGregor: Edward Hyde's younger sister stands alongside a tree and plaque erected at the inauguration of the Merchant Navy Convoy Grove in Alrewas, Staffs on the 1st October 1998. Tree 767, Area 22 is dedicated to Edward Hyde and those lost onboard *SS Peterton*. *(Isabel McGregor - Private Collection)*

Freetown (King Tom) Cemetery Today:
Where the body of Edward Briggs Hyde rests today. Cemetery Plot 7.Grave E 5. He is one of 527 Allied casualties to be buried at this site. *(www.cwgc.org)*

The greatest psychological barrier that many merchant seamen faced during World War Two was that a U-boat could strike them at any moment during their voyage, even in sight of land and even in the midst of a well escorted convoy.

J. A. Morley: 'I would not say I was afraid – let's just say I was a light sleeper!'

When the war was over, anxiety was not always replaced by the tranquillity offered by peace but instead by a sagging depression. The attrition to the human mind caused by long-term anxiety and a failure to come to terms with the traumatic consequences of war meant that many merchant seamen suffered terribly in the years that followed.

A sentiment was shared by many returning merchant seamen was that their so called non-combative jobs were less worthy than other members of the armed forces. The reality is that the Merchant Navy suffered appalling casualties similar to most branches of the armed forces. The total number of human casualties on British merchant vessels is estimated to be around 35,000, just 35-40% less than the Royal Navy who lost 51,578. The Army lost 177,580 and the Royal Air Force 76,342.

Jack Morley survived the war and settled down to a normal life and married his sweetheart, Barbara, who he met when he was nineteen.

Jimmy Meeks suffered from a hearing defect, and although he often attributed the condition to his lifeboat voyage, it was, according to his family, as much as he ever said about the war.

Frank Nock of Hull, who did so much to help George

Howes in the lifeboat and received The British Empire Medal, became Jimmy Meeks' lifelong friend. Jack Morley also maintained contact with Frank Nock after the war but they never discussed their war experiences. What we do know is that many of the men chose not to talk publicly about their traumatic war experiences, family and friends knew little or nothing of their lifeboat voyage, they did not ask for sympathy and they certainly did not bask in glory. The memories may have been just too traumatic. 2nd Officer George Howes, whose actions saved the lives of many of the *Peterton*'s crew, passed away in 1961 aged 62.

That boys like Jimmy and Teddy may have been driven by the financial rewards should not be overlooked, the money must have felt like a small fortune to them at the time. Some sailors 'did it for the money' and did not join the Merchant Navy to see the world. However, I am convinced that they held true to their original motives for joining the Merchant Navy – they sought adventure and they found adventure.

Jack Baron: Jimmy Meeks and I had some great times together in the Merchant Navy. We especially enjoyed our spells ashore where parties were often arranged for us by the Army. They'd play the latest hit songs and we'd sing along and be singing them on the ship for days afterwards. I lost contact with Jimmy after the war and often wondered what had happened to him. I even tried to contact him by leaving messages on Merchant Navy forums. It was only when I spoke to Jack Morley that I learned of Jimmy's death.

Jimmy Meeks sailed on into peacetime with hardly a

break in between. He was reunited with Captain Thomas Marrie in November 1948 on Chapman's SS Brighton. Following his release from Milag, Marrie had returned to sea soon after in August 1945 as Master of the Empire Dominica. No doubt he and Jimmy had plenty to talk about.

Jimmy Meeks left SS Brighton and R. Chapman and Son in November 1949 and, after a couple of years of freelancing, started working for James Fisher & Sons Ltd. of Barrow in 1951. He worked his way up in rank and in 1954, at the age of 28, became Master of M/V Sound Fisher, earning the right to be known as The Old Man. He skippered several of the James Fisher & Sons fleet, including M/V Bay Fisher. In 1960, he took command of the Marchon Trader. His last voyage as Master was in December 1963. In 1965 Jimmy Meeks became a Trinity House Pilot for the ports of Workington and Whitehaven on the west coast of England. Trinity House pilots can boast of their association with an institution bearing a history that goes back to 1514, when it was founded by Henry VIII to regulate piloting activities on the river Thames. It was a job to be proud of and I was proud to see my uncle at work. He would don his overcoat and trademark beret and he would make the short journey to Workington or Whitehaven. Workington and Whitehaven served as ports for the northwest's coal industry but neither could be described as large. Larger vessels had to be skilfully manoeuvred around impossible bends in the harbour using only ropes and the dockside bollards as anchor points.

I often joined him at work during my summer holidays in the Seventies. Sometimes we would be in the pilot boat making the short trip out to an awaiting cargo ship where Jimmy would expertly time his leap onto the scramble net hanging precariously over the side of the awaiting ship; or we would be waiting for him when he had successfully manoeuvred a ship out of the harbour, where he would perform the equally hazardous task of leaping from the ship's scramble net onto the deck of the pilot boat. He liked to remind me that he had never fallen overboard. It is quite telling that he made a point of this but never once mentioned that he had spent 49 days in an open lifeboat in the mid-Atlantic.

We made our last trip together on the pilot boat in 1982. I was sixteen-years-old, and not much older than Jimmy was when he first went to sea. We joined the pilot boat in Workington Harbour and I was introduced to its skipper, Charlie. He welcomed me warmly and then seemed to forget I was there as the air turned blue as he chatted to Jimmy. Later, Jimmy took me quietly to one-side and apologised on behalf of his errant colleague. He then boarded the cargo ship that was now ready to depart. Charlie steered the pilot boat and its 16-year-old passenger out of the harbour and into the Irish Sea. Steep blue-grey rollers filled the wheelhouse window and it became obvious we were in for a rough ride. I had only ever been invited along before when the temperamental Irish Sea was considered calm enough; I was soon wishing I had stayed at home. The pilot boat began to adopt that awful repetitive rocking motion as it fought against the oncoming waves and I was soon entering the miserable world of the seasick. Sweat began pouring out of my body like I had swamp fever. I needed a cold drink, but there was no water. The rising temperature and the ever-present smell of diesel fumes made sitting in the deck cabin quite unbearable so I relocated to the aft deck where the air was cool and a lot fresher. The reprieve was only temporary: as we ventured even further out to sea, the swell increased and I was soon clinging to the cabin railings to avoid being catapulted over the side. I struggled back inside and resigned myself to an hour of misery. The welcome sight of my uncle hopping back down onto the deck meant that I was able to comfort myself in the knowledge that we would soon be home. As he entered the wheelhouse, I muttered that I wasn't feeling too well. He gave a sympathetic nod but after forty years at sea he knew that no amount of comforting would change anything. Worse was to come, for some reason we seemed to be sailing northwards, away from Workington and into the Solway Firth. 'Why are we heading for Scotland?' I wondered, too disheartened to ask.

Later, as we finally chugged into some unknown Scottish harbour, I was surprised to see Jimmy's car parked on the instantly familiar quayside – we were back in Workington! I was elated, having made it back to port without being sick, and silently relieved that I hadn't embarrassed Jimmy and myself by asking what we were doing in Scotland. I had gone to hell and back in less than an hour. The memory of that day put Jimmy's 49 day lifeboat voyage into its true and brutal perspective.

Jimmy Meeks died in 1988 aged 62, a victim of cancer, a disease that also claimed his brother, John, in 1983 aged only 47. Jimmy's wife, Peggy Meeks, passed away in 2004. His sisters, Margaret and Eva, now in their seventies, still live in the north-east.

Jack Morley is the only living survivor from the *Peterton* the author has been able to trace. He lives at home with his wife Barbara in Hull. We call each other from time to time and talk about his life in the Merchant Navy.

Jimmy Meeks was only 19-years old when the war ended on the 8th May 1945. He had survived eight Atlantic crossings, made port in countries as diverse as Algeria, Italy, Canada, Gibraltar and Argentina, sailed in twelve convoys, been subjected to U-boat attacks on three separate occasions, shipwrecked on his first voyage, drifted 49 days in an open lifeboat and lost many friends and colleagues. Technically still an apprentice and, by the war's end, a veteran.

11. APPENDIX I. WAR SERVICE RECORD - JAMES NICHOLSON MEEKS

M.N.R.P SS *PETERTON* – ON. 142854

Date	Convoy	From	To	Date	Cargo	Notes
24.08.42		Hull	Methil	27.08.42		
28.08.42		Methil	Oban	01.09.42		
01.09.42	OG89	Oban	Buenos Aires (Freetown)	17.09.42		Ship attacked and sunk by U-109 north-west Azores. Picked up by HMT Canna 04.11.42 after 49 days adrift.
Unknown		Freetown	Newcastle	07.12.42		Repatriated. No convoys in this period.

TRANSFERED TO SS *GENERTON* ON. 161600

Date	Convoy	From	To	Date	Cargo	Notes
30.01.43		Tyne	Methil	31.01.43		Jimmy Meeks musters on 19.01.43
02.02.43		Methil Greenock	Clyde/	05.02.43		BT 389/13: Delayed sailing due to bad weather
06.03.43	OS44	Clyde	Gibraltar	16.03.43	Coal	Convoy attacked by U-107. Five ships sunk. BT 389/13: Awaiting orders – 19/03
24.03.43		Gibraltar	Algiers (Alg)	27.03.43		
03.04.43		Algiers (Alg)	Bone (Alg) (Annaba)	04.04.43		

Date	Convoy	From	To	Date	Cargo	Notes
18.04.43		Bone (Alg) (Annaba)	Bougie (Alg) (Bejaïa)	19.04.43		
28.04.43		Bougie (Alg) (Bejaïa)	Gibraltar	02.05.43		
22.05.43		Gibraltar	Loch Ewe	01.06.43		
02.06.43		Loch Ewe	Methil	04.06.43		
04.06.43		Methil	Middlesboro	05.06.43		
05.06.43		Middlesboro	Tyne	07.06.43		BT 389/13: 15/06 Tyne – Repairs completed 24/06
24.06.43		Tyne	Methil	24.06.43		
25.06.43		Methil	Oban	28.06.43		
04.07.43	*ONS12	Oban	Halifax	18.07.43		Ballast First Atlantic crossing for Jimmy Meeks
24.07.43		Halifax	Sydney (Can)	26.07.43		
27.07.43		Sydney (Can)	Corner Brook (Can)	28.07.43		
28.07.43		Corner Brook (Can)	Sydney (Can)	06.08.43		BT 389/13: Repairs in Corner Brook completed 06/08
10.08.43	*SC139 or HX251	Sydney (Can)	Loch Ewe	25.08.43	Wood-Pulp	Atlantic Convoy (East)

Date	Convoy	From	To	Date	Cargo	Notes
25.08.43		Loch Ewe	Methil	26.08.43		
27.08.43		Methil	London	29.08.43		BT 389/13: Passed St Abbs Head 27/08
10.09.43		London	Southend	10.09.43		
11.09.43		Southend	Tyne	13.09.43		
16.09.43		Tyne	Methil	16.09.43		
17.09.43		Methil	Oban	20.09.43		
27.09.43	*ONS19 or ON204	Oban	Sydney (Can)	13.10.43		Atlantic Convoy (West)
14.10.43		Sydney (Can)	Halifax (Can)	15.10.43		
??.10.43		Halifax (Can)	Sydney (Can)	??.10.43		
27.10.43		Sydney (Can)	Corner Brook (Can)	28.10.43		
09.11.44		Corner Brook (Can)	Sydney (Can)	11.11.43		
20.11.43	*SC147 or HX267	Sydney (Can)	Loch Ewe	04.12.43	Timber/ Steel	Atlantic Convoy (East)
04.12.43		Loch Ewe	Methil	06.12.43		

Date	Convoy	From	To	Date	Cargo	Notes
07.12.43		Methil	Tyne	08.12.42		BT 389/13: Passed St Abbs Head 07/12
09.12.43		Tyne	Rochester	12.12.43		
23.12.43		Rochester (London)	Hull	25.12.43		BT 389/13: Repairs completed in Hull 08/01
08.01.44		Hull	Methil	10.01.44		BT 389/13: Passed Spurn Head 09.01.44, St Abbs Head 10.01.44
12.01.44		Methil	Loch Ewe	14.01.44		
14.01.44	OS65/KMS39	Aultbea (Loch Ewe)	Catania (Sicily)	03.02.44	Potatoes/Vehicles	Convoy attacked by U-641 – U-boat sunk by HMS Violet
13.02.44		Catania (Sicily)	Augusta (Sicily)	13.02.44		
14.02.44		Augusta (Sicily)	Philippeville (Alg) (Skikda)	18.02.44		BT 389/13: Bound for Gibraltar but put into Philippeville (Algeria) due to Boiler defects.
22.02.44		Philippeville (Alg) (Skikda)	Gibraltar	26.02.44		

212

TRANSFERED TO SS *GRAINTON* ON. 149489

Date	Convoy	From	To	Date	Cargo	Notes
22.03.44	*MKS-43G R/V SL152	Gibraltar	Loch Ewe	03.04.44		02.03.44 – Grainton arrived in Gibraltar and undergoes repairs to lifeboats and davit arms. 11.03.44 - Jimmy Meeks musters on Grainton in Gibraltar. BT 389/14: Directed to London 30/3.
04.04.44		Loch Ewe	Methil	06.04.44		
07.04.44		Methil	Southend	19.04.44		
20.04.44		Southend	Grangemouth	22.04.44		BT 389/14: Via St Abbs
22.04.44		Grangemouth	Methil	01.05.44		
02.05.44		Methil	S. Shields	03.05.44		BT 389/14: Ship enters Tyne for repairs. Jimmy Meeks musters off. Completed 17/07
19.07.44		S. Shields	Methil	20.07.44		
22.07.44		Methil	Loch Ewe	24.07.44		
25.07.44		Loch Ewe	Greenock	27.07.44		BT 389/14: Put back - engine trouble. Repairs comp 01/08
02.08.44	*ON247	Greenock	Montreal (Can)	15.08.44		Convoy probably ON247 as ONS convoys suspended as escorts were diverted to Normandy landings

Date	Convoy	From	To	Date	Cargo	Notes
20.08.44		Montreal	Sydney (Can)	23.08.44		
03.09.44	HX306	Sydney (Can)	Hull	21.09.44	Grain	Atlantic Convoy (East). BT 389/14: Sailed for Loch Ewe but diverted to Hull- via Southend (18/9). Repairs completed 22.09.44
02.10.44		Hull	Hull	03.10.44		BT 389/14: Put back - engine trouble
04.10.44		Hull	S. Shields	05.10.44		BT 389/14: Tyne – repairs completed 13/10
13.10.44		S. Shields	Methil	14.10.44		
14.10.44		Methil	Methil	17.10.44		Grainton left Methil for three days but BT 389/14 does not state its destination
21.10.44		Methil	Loch Ewe	24.10.44		
29.10.44	*ONS35 or ON263	Loch Ewe	Sorel	19.11.44		BT 389/14: Boiler repairs - completed 02/12
02.12.44		Sorel (Can)	Quebec (Can)	02.12.44		
02.12.44		Quebec (Can)	Sydney (Can)	05.12.44		
17.12.44	SC163	Sydney (Can)	Loch Ewe	31.12.44	Grain	Atlantic Convoy (East)

Date	Convoy	From	To	Date	Cargo	Notes
01.01.45		Loch Ewe	Methil	03.01.45		
04.01.45		Methil	Southend	07.01.45		BT 389/14: Anchored
18.01.45		Southend	S. Shields	21.01.45		22.01.45 - Jimmy Meeks musters on Grainton BT 389/14: Repairs at Tyne completed 10/3.
14.03.45		S. Shields	Southend	16.03.45	BT 389/14: Transfers grain.	
17.03.45		Southend	Rosario (Arg)	18.04.45		
26.04.45		Rosario (Arg)	Buenos Aires (Arg)	27.04.45		
05.05.45		Buenos Aires	Gibraltar	02.06.45		VE Day 8th May 1945 celebrated at sea!
02.06.45		Gibraltar	Barry	08.06.45		
08.06.45		Barry	Avonmouth	10.06.45		
20.06.45		Avonmouth	Barry	20.06.45		Jimmy Meeks musters off

12. APPENDIX II. LIST OF THE CREW: SS PETERTON

#	Name	Age	Nationality/ Birthplace	Discharge Number	Date/Place of Agreement	Capacity	Date of Joining	Particulars of Discharge	Cause
1	Thomas William Marrie *	33	Sunderland		17.08.42 Hull	Master	17.08.42	17.09.42 At Sea*	Prisoner
2	Francis Buller Fairweather 2 • King's Commendation	42	East Ham	R1029837	18.08.42 Hull	1st Mate	17.08.42	17.09.42 Newcastle	Discharged
3	George Denis Howes 1 • George Medal	43	Hull	A910075	18.08.42 Hull	2nd Mate	18.08.42	17.09.42 Newcastle	Discharged
4	Ernest Benjamin Thompson 1	32	Norfolk	R42608	21.08.42 Hull	3rd Mate	17.08.42	17.09.42 Newcastle	Discharged
5	Jonathan Islwyn Davies 1 • King's Commendation	30	Goodwich	R155565	18.08.42 Hull	1st Radio Officer	17.08.42	17.09.42 Newcastle	Discharged
6	Thomas Alfred White ▼	30	Hull	R226985	21.08.42 Hull	2nd Radio Officer	at once	17.09.42 At Sea	Missing

#	Name	Age	Nationality/ Birthplace	Discharge Number	Date/Place of Agreement	Capacity	Date of Joining	Particulars of Discharge	Cause
7	John S. Watt 1	59	Lerwick	R926091	18.08.42 Hull	Bosun	19.08.42	17.09.42 Newcastle	Discharged
8	Francis Nock 1 • British Empire Medal	20	Hull	R220079	18.08.42 Hull	Able Seaman	19.08.42	17.09.42 Newcastle	Discharged
9	George Raymond Norfolk 2	27	Hull	R147597	18.08.42 Hull	Able Seaman	19.08.42	17.09.42 Newcastle	Discharged
10	George Thomas Pennington 1	19	Wigan	R231168	18.08.42 Hull	Sailor	19.08.42	17.09.42 Newcastle	Discharged
1	George Keay 2	19	Hull	R216951	18.08.42 Hull	Sailor	19.08.42	17.09.42 Newcastle	Discharged
12	John Ennis 1	47	Wexford	R147308 1	8.08.42 Hull	Sailor	19.08.42	17.09.42 Newcastle	Discharged
13	James Henry Stephenson 2	22	Hull	R195507	18.08.42 Hull	Ordinary Seaman	19.08.42	17.09.42 Newcastle	Discharged
14	John Albert Morley 2	18	Hull	R216997	18.08.42 Hull	Ordinary Seaman	19.08.42	17.09.42 Newcastle	Discharged

#	Name	Age	Nationality/ Birthplace	Discharge Number	Date/Place of Agreement	Capacity	Date of Joining	Particulars of Discharge	Cause
15	Thomas Cuthbert Gorman 1 • OBE	44	No. Shields	R1029045	18.08.42 Hull	1st Eng	17.08.42	17.09.42 Newcastle	Discharged
16	Robert Morrison Gardiner ▼	50	So. Shields	R734275	21.08.42 Hull	2nd Eng	20.08.42	17.09.42 At sea	Missing
17	Henry William Runnacles ▼	49	Hull	R189891	22.08.42 Hull	3rd Eng	20.08.42	17.09.42 At sea	Missing
18	Walter March ▼	20	Hull		22.08.42 Hull	4th Eng	20.08.42	17.09.42 At sea	Missing
19	Albert A. Hoe Richardson 1	39	Hull	R211179	20.08.42 Hull	Greaser	at once	17.09.42 Newcastle	Discharged
20	George Johnson ▼	25	Hull	R150473	18.08.42 Hull	Donkeyman	20.08.42	17.09.42 At sea	Missing
21	Hugh Patrick Gray ▼	50	Belfast	R966868	19.08.42 Hull	Fireman & Trimmer	21.08.42	17.09.42 At sea	Missing
22	Raymond Alfred Tennant ▼	24	York	R251620	19.08.42 Hull	Fireman & Trimmer	20.08.42	17.09.42 At sea	Missing
23	Samuel Osborne 1	31	Hull	R234400	19.08.42 Hull	Fireman & Trimmer	21.08.42	17.09.42 Newcastle	Discharged

#	Name	Age	Nationality/ Birthplace	Discharge Number	Date/Place of Agreement	Capacity	Date of Joining	Particulars of Discharge	Cause
24	Charles Edward Johnson Smith 2	19	Hull	R251621	19.08.42 Hull	Fireman & Trimmer	21.08.42	17.09.42 Newcastle	Discharged
25	Hati Chand 1	24	Trinidad		19.08.42 Hull	Fireman & Trimmer	21.08.42	17.09.42 Newcastle	Discharged
26	James Eric Green ▼	20	Hull	R220903	19.08.42 Hull	Fireman & Trimmer	21.08.42	17.09.42 At sea	Missing
27	Alan M. Goodfellow 2	18	Hull	R318746	19.08.42 Hull	Fireman & Trimmer	21.08.42	17.09.42 Newcastle	Discharged
28	H. Johansson	61	SWEDEN 1		9.08.42 Hull	Fireman & Trimmer	21.08.42	21.08.42 Hull	Failed to join
29	Herbert Weaver 2	34	Hull		19.08.42 Hull	Fireman & Trimmer	21 108.42	17.09.42 Newcastle	Discharged
30	Archibald Morrison Swan 1	33	Sunderland		19.08.42 Hull	Chief Steward	17.08.42	17.09.42 Newcastle	Discharged
31	J. M. Taylor	25	Grimsby		20.08.42 Cook	Hull Ship's	at once	21.08.42 Hull	Deserted
32	H. Elsworthy	17	Hull		19.08.42 Hull	Galley Boy	20.08.42	20.08.42 Hull	Discharged

#	Name	Age	Nationality/ Birthplace	Discharge Number	Date/Place of Agreement	Capacity	Date of Joining	Particulars of Discharge	Cause
33	Reginald Harrison 1	17	Scunthorpe	R270404	19.08.42 Hull	Mess R Boy	20.08.42	17.09.42 Newcastle	Discharged
34	Dennis Harold Thirkettle 1	19	Hull	R269016	19.08.42 Hull	Cabin Boy	20.08.42	17.09.42 Newcastle	Discharged
35	William Tresedder Lytle 2	33	Belfast		18.08.42 Hull	Deck Hand/DEMS	17.08.42	17.09.42 Newcastle	Discharged
36	W. E. Lambie 1	28	Bristol	R191339	21.08.42 Hull	Deck Hand/DEMS	at once	17.09.42 Newcastle	Discharged
37	Albert Verdun Lewington 1	25	London	A.6086357	18.08.42 Hull	Deck Hand/DEMS	14.08.42	17.09.42 Newcastle	Discharged
38	Sydney Ludlam 1	21	Sheffield	S11423943	18.08.42 Hull	Deck Hand/DEMS	14.08.42	17.09.42 Newcastle	Discharged
39	Joseph Derbyshire	36	Blackburn		18.08.42 Hull	Deck Hand	14.08.42	20.08.42 Hull	Discharged
40	Michael Sexton	34	Rhymney		18.08.42 Hull	Deck Hand	14.08.42	20.08.42 Hull	Discharged
41	Albert William Hickling 1	35	Leicester	P/JX 312766	21.08.42 Hull	Deck Hand/DEMS		17.09.42 Newcastle	Discharged

#	Name	Age	Nationality/ Birthplace	Discharge Number	Date/Place of Agreement	Capacity	Date of Joining	Particulars of Discharge	Cause
42	Ronald Minnery 1	21	Caterham	D/JX 254330	21.08.42 Hull	Deck Hand/DEMS	at once	17.09.42 Newcastle	Discharged
43	William Brooks 2	18	Preston		21.08.42 Hull	Deck Hand/DEMS	at once	17.09.42 Newcastle	Discharged
44	Michael Byrne 2	17	Goole	R240947	24.08.42 Hull	Galley Boy	22.08.42	17.09.42 Newcastle	Discharged
45	William Haughton 2	22	Methil	R147707	27.08.42 Methil	Fireman	26.08.42	17.09.42 Newcastle	Discharged
46	Geo Fisher 1	34	Sunderland	R80992	28.08.42 Methil	Cook	at once	17.09.42	Discharged
APP	Edward Briggs Hyde 1 ▼ • King's Commendation	15	Cullercoats		21.08.42 Hull	Apprentice	21.08.42	17.09.42 Freetown	Died 16th Nov Pneumonia
APP	James Nicholson Meeks 1 • King's Commendation	16	So. Shields	R285751	24.08.42 Hull	Apprentice	24.08.42	17.09.42 Newcastle	Discharged

1 = Starboard Lifeboat, 2 = Port Lifeboat, ▼ = Killed in Action, • = Bravery Award

13. APPENDIX III. LIST OF THE CREW: U-109

Surname	First Name	Rank German	Born	Died	Notes:
Anelzberger	Siegfried	ObStrm	12.02.1913	15.11.42	U-109 U-588 U-259 ▼
Arnold	Wolfgang	Mt	06.06.1921	04.05.43	U-109 ▼
Bender	Karl	Gfr	27.06.1923	04.05.43	U-109 ▼
Benzmann	Walter	Mt	30.09.1919	04.05.43	U-109 ▼
Berkemeier	Friedrich	Gfr	20.05.1924	04.05.43	U-109 ▼
Bischoff	Jürgen	FkMt			U-109
Bleichrodt	Heinrich	KKpt	21.10.1909	09.01.1977	U8 U34 U48 U109
Bocker	Gerhard	Mt	23.07.1921	04.05.43	U-109 ▼
Borchardt	Werner	BtsMt			U-109
Boss	Kurt	Obgfr	12.04.1921	04.05.43	U-109 ▼
Braatz	Wilhelm	Obstrm	06.01.1916	04.05.43	U-109 ▼
Breuckmann	Josef				U-109 U-233
Breuer	Matthias	MechMt			U-109
Bruns	Helmut	Lt	04.06.1921	04.05.43	U-109 ▼
Christossek	Gunter	Obgfr	27.08.1923	04.05.43	U-109 ▼
Detzner	Herbert	Lt	17.12.1923	04.05.43	U-109 ▼
Eichler	Gastav	Mt	21.07.1923	04.05.43	U-109 ▼
Engmann.	Herb	ObMasch	05.05.1917	04.05.43	U-109 ▼
Feil	Heinrich	ObGfr	14.06.1922	04.05.43	U-109 ▼
Fischer	Hans-Georg	FKapt	03.02.1908		U-109 Adm. Scheer, Hansa
Flegel	Hans-Jurgen	ObGfr	26.06.1923	04.05.43	U-109 ▼
Geisser	Karl	ObGfr	09.08.1922	04.05.43	U-109 ▼
Goldbeck	Herbert -Heinrich	MtrOGfr	31.03.1922	04.05.43	U-109 ▼
Gross	Walter	Obmt	17.12.1916	08.10.43	U-109 U-460 ▼
Habicht	Jurgen	Lt	14.08.1920	04.05.43	U-109 ▼
Hagen	Ferdinand	FkOGfr	21.07.1919	04.05.43	U-109 ▼
Heil	Heinz	MaschOGfr	14.08.1920	04.05.43	U-109 ▼
Hengen	Dieter	Olt.z.S	19.10.1922		U-109 U-2364
Hentschel	Heinz	ObMt	11.02.1917	04.05.43	U-109 ▼
Heyer	Albert	Lt.ig	13.11.1920	04.05.43	U-109 ▼
Hirschfeld	Wolfgang	ObFkMt	20.05.1916	20.05.2005	U-109 U-234
Hoffmann	Eberhard	FKapt	16.05.1907	27.09.1942	U-109 U-165 ▼
Holzapfel	Heinrich	MaschOGfr	20.02.1923	04.05.1943	U-109 ▼
Jackel	Richard	ObGfr	26.02.1923	04.05.43	U-109 ▼
Järschel	Werner	MtrOGfr			U-109
Jürgensen	Hein				U-109

Surname	First Name	Rank German	Born	Died	Notes:
Keller	Siegfried	ObLt.2WO	30.10.1917	12.03.43	U-109 U-38 U130 ▼
Kindermann	Wilhelm	ObMasch	12.01.1917	04.05.43	U-109 ▼
Klein	Manfred	Gfr	19.02.1923	04.05.43	U-109 ▼
Kolzapfel	Heinrich	ObGfr	20.02.1923	04.05.43	U-109 ▼
Korn	Berthold	Gfr	13.12.1924	04.05.43	U-109 ▼
Lechner	Alfons	Gfr	02.08.1923	04.05.43	U-109 ▼
Lenz	Kurt	Gfr	20.02.1923	04.05.43	U-109 ▼
Leyes	Aloys	ObGfr	09.12.1921	04.05.43	U-109 ▼
Liekefett	Wilhelm	Gfr	29.07.1923	04.05.43	U-109 ▼
Lindert	Kurt	Fährr. Z.S			U-109 + 7 boats
Loose	Georg	ObGfr	21.06.1924	04.05.43	U-109 ▼
Lüttge	Willi	MtrOGfr	03.11.1920	04.05.43	U-109 ▼
Lusch	Gerhard	Gfr	20.04.1923	04.05.43	U-109 ▼
Mäck	Karl	ObMt	06.06.1919	04.05.43	U-109 ▼
Maureschat	Eduard	BtsMt	16.01.1917	31.05.2006	U-109
Monecke	Walter	Mech			U-109 U-986
Moritz	Werner	OMasch	23.03.1914		U-106 U-109
Morsel	Helmut	Mt	21.07.1923	04.05.43	U-109 ▼
Muck	Kurt	Obgfr	23.01.1924	04.05.43	U-109 ▼
Nickolai	Anton	MaschMt	10.01.1916	04.05.43	U-109 ▼
Peters	Otto				U-109
Petersen	Bruno				U-109
Pötter	Paul	Btsmt	10.01.1922		U-109 U-859
Reichert	Günter	MaschGfr	07.07.1921	04.05.43	U-109 ▼
Reissnauer	Karl	ObMaschMt			U-109
Reiter	Karl	Gfr	25.06.1924	04.05.43	U-109 ▼
Rieger	Friedrich	ObGfr	06.06.1920	04.05.43	U-109 ▼
Salewski	Herbert	Mt	26.02.1921	04.05.43	U-109 ▼
Sallach	Walter	Gfr	06.02.1925	04.05.43	U-109 ▼
Salzer	Hans	Gfr	04.04.1923	04.05.43	U-109 ▼
Schaufel	Gerhard	MaschOGfr	26.01.1924	04.05.43	U-109 ▼
Schewe		OMasch			U-109
Schramm	Joachim	ObLt.Cdr	03.06.1916	04.05.43	U-109 ▼
Schwartzkopf	Volker	ObLt	25.04.1914	04.05.43	U-109 U-107 U-520 ▼
Seidel	Berthold	BtsMt			U-109
Seiler	Willy	MachMt			U-109
Spenner	Friedrich	ObGfr	18.02.1921	04.05.43	U-109 ▼
Staffeldt	Wolfgang	ObGfr	12.09.1921	04.05.43	U-109 ▼
Strasseberger	Max	ObGfr	20.06.1922	04.05.43	U-109 ▼
Vetter	Walter	ObMt	06.07.1914	04.05.43	U-109 ▼

Surname	First Name	Rank German	Born	Died	Notes:
Wagenhofer	Peter-Alois	Mtr.I			U-109 U-1024
Weber	Martin	KpLt.ing	26.01.1916	04.05.43	U-109 U-526 ▼
Wenzel	Kuddel				U-109 U-522 ▼
Wex	Hans-Dieter	Olt.z.S	05.09.1920	12.08.1989	U-109 + 6 boats
Wiegle	Walter	Mt	08.06.1921	14.04.43	U-109 ▼
Will	Karl	MtrGfr			U-109 UD-2 U-1052
Winter	Alfred	Ing			U-109
Wissmann	Friedrich-Wilhelm	KpLt	16.12.1915	09.09.1963	U-109 U18 U-518
Witte	Werner	KpLt.	05.01.1915	15.07.1943	U-109 U-509
Wittfeld	Herbert	Gfr	10.05.1922	04.05.43	U-109 ▼
Zank	Karl	Mt	27.05.1921	04.05.43	U-109 ▼

▼ *indicates died while crew of boat*

14. APPENDIX IV. TECHNICAL INFORMATION FOR U-109 TYPE IXB

Other U-boats of this type:
U-64, U-65, U-103, U-104, U-105, U-106, U-107, U-108, U-110, U-111, U-122, U-123, and U-124.

Displacement: (tons)	1051 (surface) 1178 (submerged) 1430 (total)	Speed: (knots) Range: (miles/knots)	18,2 (surface) 7,3 (submerged) 12,000/10 (surface) 64/4 (submerged)
Length: (metres)	76,50 (overall) 58,75 (pressure hull)	Torpedoes:	22 4/2 (bow/stern tubes)
Beam: (metres)	6,76 (overall) 4,40 (pressure hull)	Mines:	44 TMA
Draught:	4,70 m	Deck gun:	105/45 110 rounds
Height:	9,60 m	Crew:	48-56 men
Power: (horse power)	4,400 (surfaced) 1,000 (submerged)	Max depth:	230 m (755 feet)

U-109 Kyffhauser Association Lighthouse Emblem 1941: Heinrich Bleichrodt brought this emblem with him from U-67 and it featured on U-109's conning tower during early patrols in 1941. (*Embleme, Wappen, Malings Deutscher U-boote 1939 –1945: Georg Høgel*)

U-109 Kyffhauser Association Lighthouse Emblem 1942: This later emblem featured on U-109's conning tower during their sixth patrol and would have been visible to the crew of Peterton when U-109 pulled alongside their lifeboat. (*Embleme, Wappen, Malings Deutscher U-boote 1939–1945: Georg Høgel*)

U-109 belonged to 2nd U-boat flotilla *Saltzwedel*. Founded on 1st Sept 1936 under the command of Fregkpt. Scheer. From June 1940 to June 1941 the flotilla moved to Lorient, France. Its history ended in August 1944 when the last boats left Lorient for Norway. (*Embleme, Wappen, Malings Deutscher U-boote 1939–1945: Georg Høgel*)

U-109 Class Symbol painted on the conning tower designates it as a Type IX U-boat manufactured at Deschimag, Bremen. (*Embleme, Wappen, Malings Deutscher U-boote 1939–1945: Georg Høgel*)

15. APPENDIX V. GALLANTRY AWARDS DURING THE SECOND WORLD WAR (MERCHANT NAVY)

Official gallantry awards are classified as being in four levels that relate to the estimated risk of loss of life to the recipient, in attempting their gallant act(s): 'I' being the highest level, and 'IV' the lowest.

Gallantry Awards during the Second World War (Merchant Navy)
Bernard de Neumann, The City University, London

Award	Level	No
George Cross	I	4
Empire Gallantry Medal	I	1
Knighthood	*	10
Commander of the Order of the British Empire	III	50
Officer of the Order of the British Empire	III	1077
Member of the Order of the British Empire	III	1291
Distinguished Service Order	II	14
Distinguished Cross	III	213
Albert Cross	I to II	10
George Medal	II	49
Distinguished Service Medal	III	421
Sea Gallantry Medal	III	24
British Empire Medal	III	1717
Mentions in Despatches	IV	994
Commendations (James Meeks and Edward Hyde)	IV	2568
Lloyd's War Medal for Bravery at Sea	I to IV	530
Total		8973

The Empire Gallantry Medal was revoked by Royal Warrant in favour of the George Cross on 24 September 1940. All living E.G.M. recipients had to exchange them for the George Cross. A further Royal Warrant of 15 December 1971 revoked the Albert Medal, and all living recipients were deemed to be holders of the George Cross, and offered the opportunity to exchange their Albert Medal for a George Cross Not all took the opportunity.

War Medal (1939–1945). Awarded to all whose service included at least 28 days at sea, or whose service was terminated by death, injury, or capture. Ribbon denotes the colours of the Union Flag.

Bronze Oak Leaf. This emblem is for a mention in dispatches, or the King's Commendation for brave conduct and is attached to the War Medal ribbon. Only one emblem is worn no matter how many times a person may have been mentioned.

1939–1945 Star. Awarded for six months service afloat, which had to include at least one voyage in the theatre of war. The dark blue ribbon represents the Royal & Merchant Navies, red the Army, and light blue for the RAF.

Atlantic Star. Awarded for six months at sea with at least one voyage in the prescribed area of operations. Also for service on the Russian Convoys, and fast unescorted Merchant ships. The ribbon colours are watered and shaded to represent the Atlantic Ocean.

Africa Star 1940-43. Awarded for any service in the Mediterranean or off the Horn of Africa. The buff colour ribbon represents desert sand, dark blue for both Navies, red represents the Army and light blue represents the RAF.

Lloyd's War Medal for Bravery at Sea.
In 1939, with the advance of World War II, Lloyd's set up a committee to find a means of honouring seafarers who performed acts of exceptional courage at sea and this resulted in the announcement in December 1940 of the Lloyd's War Medal for Bravery at Sea. The first awards were announced in March 1941, and the last in October 1948, all awards were for acts during the Second World War. In all 541 Lloyd's War Medals for Bravery at Sea were awarded.

16. REFERENCES

Unpublished Sources:

National Archives, Kew, London:

Shipping Casualty Report for *SS Peterton* R.T.D.139.1629. 8th January 1943
BT 381/1866 1942 Jan 01 – Dec 31
SS Peterton 1942 – BT373/249
Registry of Shipping and Seamen: Central Register of Seamen: Seamen's Records ('Pouches') – BT372
Memorandum from 'The Commanding Officer H.M.T. Canna to The Captain', Auxiliary Patrol – ADM 199/1276
Particulars of Attacks on Merchant Vessels by Enemy Submarines – ADM 199/1272
SS Peterton Official Log Books and Telegrams BT381/1866
SS Generton Official Log Books BT381/2479
Ship Movement Log for SS Generton BT389/13
Ship Movement Log for SS Generton BT389/16 (Summary)
Ship Movement Log for SS Grainton BT389/14
Seaman's Service Record – James Nicholson Meeks BT382/1209
Seaman's Service Record – Thomas William Marrie BT382/1179
Seaman's Identity Cards– James Nicholson Meeks BT372/1332/57
Cruising Order – Mercantile Convoy OS44 – ADM237/151
Cruising Order – Mercantile Convoy OG89 – ADM237/61
Cruising Order – Mercantile Convoy OS65/KMS65

Register of Apprentices Indentures
Merchant Navy Gallantry Awards Log
Registry of Shipping and Seamen: War of 1939-1945;
　Merchant Seamen
Prisoner of War Records: Thomas William Marrie
　BT373/249
Tyne & Wear Archive: Chapman and Willan Ltd. Voyage
　Ledger SS Generton
1475/1-75

Newspapers, Periodicals, Charts and Broadcasts:

International Express (Australia) page 24, 10th February
　2004. *'Reminiscing With The Enemy.'*
Shields Gazette and Shipping Telegraph, January 1943.
McCance, R.A., Ungley, C.C,. Crosfill, C.C.W., and
　Widdowson, E.M.: *The Hazards of Men Lost to Ships at
　Sea 1939 – 1944.* Medical Research Council Special
　Report No. 291. London. HMSO. 1956.
The Times Map of The World, Sixth Edition. London. Times
　Books. 2003
The London Gazette, 11th April 1943
The London Gazette, 6th July 1943
The Daily Mail, 10th December 1942
The Evening News, 7th July 1943

<u>Literature:</u>

Barker, Ralph: *"Goodnight Sorry for Sinking You", The
　story of the SS City of Cairo.* London. Collins. 1984.

Bennett, G.H & R.: *Survivors – British Merchant Seamen in the Second World War*. London: The Hambledon Press, 1999.

Dönitz Admiral Karl: *Memoirs Ten Years and Twenty Days*. London: Cassell Military Paperbacks, 2000

Edwards, Bernard: *The Quiet Heroes: British Merchant Seamen at War*.

Edwards, Bernard: *The Fighting Tramps, The Merchant Navy Goes To War*. London. Robert Hale. 1989.

Hague, Arnold. *The Allied Convoy System 1939-1945*. Canada: Vanwell Publishing Limited 2000.

Hirschfeld, Wolfgang and Brooks, Geoffrey. *The Secret Diary of a U-boat*. London: Cassell Military Paperbacks, 2000

Högel, Georg: *Embleme Wappen Malings deutscher U-boote 1939-1945*. 4. Auflage. Hamburg. Koehlers Verlagsgesellschaft mbH. 2001

Jordan, Roger: *The World's Merchant Fleets 1939 – The Particulars and Wartime Fates of 6,000 Ships*. Annapolis, MD: Naval Institute Press, 1999.

Khan, David: *Seizing The Enigma*: London. Arrow Books Ltd. 1996.

Lennox Kerr, J. *Touching the Adventures of Merchantmen in the Second World War*. London. Harrap. 1953.

Lingwood, John & Appleyard, Harold. *Chapman of Newcastle, The Story of a Tyneside Tramp Shipping Company*. Kendal. World Ship Society. 1985.

Ministry of Information: *Merchantmen at War, The Official Story of the Merchant Navy 1939 –1944*. London. His Majesty's Stationery Office. 1944.

Murphy, Mark. [Basil Dominic Izzi.] *83 Days; The Survival of Seaman Izzi*. New York: Books, Inc.1943.

Old Ordnance Survey Map: *South Shields 1895*. The Godfrey Edition

Ritschel, Herbert: Kurzfassung Kriegstagebücher Deutscher U-boote 1939 – 1945 Band 3 KTB U100 – U124 UA UD3 UD5.

Rohwer, Jurgen. *Axis Submarine Successes of World War Two: German, Italian, and Japanese Submarine Successes, 1939-1945*. Annapolis, MD: Naval Institute Press, 1999.

Skattebol, Lars: *The Last Voyage of the Quien Sabe*. Harper & Brothers. 1944.

Stafford, David: *Roosevelt & Churchill, Men of Secrets*. London: Abacus. 1999

Tennent, Alan J. *British and Commonwealth Merchant Ship Losses to Axis Submarines 1939-1945*. Stroud: Sutton Publishing, 2001.

Thomas, Gabe: Milag, *Captives of the Kriegsmarine, Merchant Navy Prisoners of War*. Milag p.o.w. Association, Pontadarwe, 1995.

Van Der Vat, Dan: *Stealth at Sea: The History of The Submarine*: London. Orion Books. 1994

Werner, Herbert A: *Iron Coffins, A Personal Account of the German U-Boat Battles of World War II*. New York. Da Capo. 1998.

Literature in Norwegian Language:

Bjørkelund, Leif M. *Sjøfolk i Krig, Haugelendinger ser tilbake 50 år etter*. Tysvær. Skrifter fra Lokalhistorisk stiftelse. 1995.

Bøhn Per, Gjestland Trygve, Lingås Lars Gunnar. *De Seilte*

For Vår Frihet. Oslo. Grøndahl & Søn Forlag AS. 1987.
Cremer, Peter: *U-333 Kampen on Atlanteren* (norsk utgave). Oslo. 1988.
Fredh Terje *Utanför Spårran Del 1 (Atlantkonvojerna).* Swedish publication.
Juell, Harald: *En Havn På Østkysten.* Oslo. Krigsseilere, konvoier, krigsforlis. 1968.
Thowsen, Atle; Hjeltnes, Guri; Pettersen, Lauritz; Basberg, Bjørn L: *Handelsflåten i Krig 1939 –1945* (5 volumes). Oslo. Grøndahl og Dreyers Forlag A/S, 2. opplag. 1999.
Midbøe, Dag: *50 Konvoier – minner fra en krigsseiler.* Vormedal Forlag, 2008

Internet:

www.angelfire.com/de/BobSanders/
CHAPMAN SHIPS IN SERVICE 1954, CHAPMAN & WILLAN LTD. (Carlton S.S.Co. Ltd) (Cambray S.S. Co. Ltd.)
www.bbc.co.uk/ww2peopleswar/stories/44/a8824944.shtml
49 days in an open boat by Action Desk
www.blueislandivers.com Grainton dive site
www.bluestarline.org Blue Star Line
www.british-merchant-navy.co.uk British Merchant Navy
www.btinternet.com/~lawrence.woodcock/ Lawrence Woodcock – WW2 Research Specialist. Tel. 020 8878 9828. Fax 0870 1339694
www.combinedfleet.com/I-37
www.cwgc.org Commonwealth War Graves Commission
www.geocities.com/Pentagon/Camp/3166
www.lascars.co.uk/war

www.fredalaycock.org.uk Freda Laycock Memorial Web Site
www.rhaywood.karoo.net/bombmap.htm Hull Bomb Map
www.lynadair.com/ss_city_of_benares.htm The Sinking of the City Of Benares
www.mariners-l.freeserve.co.uk Researching the Mariners and Ships of the Merchant Marine and the World's Navies.
www.members.iinet.au/~gduncan/maritime-la
www.milag.org Merchant Navy Prisoners of War
www.members.tripod.com/~merchantships/ The Allied Merchant Navy of World War Two
www.merchant-navy.net Merchant Navy
www.mightyseas.co.uk/articles/awards Merchant Navy Commemorations
www.mhold.eclipse.co.uk OS and OS/KMS Convoy Series
www.rnpatrolservice.org.uk Harry Tate's Navy
www.nationalarchives.gov.uk National Archives (In co-operation with PRO)
www.naval-history.net Naval History (British losses by area)
www.plimsoll.org/images/14048_tcm4-55739.pdf Port Cities Southampton
www.portofworkington.co.uk
www.pust-norden.de Ships Photo Archives of the Shipping Company Fritzen from 1945 until 1979
www.searcher.dircon.co.uk/index.htm R.W. O'Hara – National Archive Searches, 15 Ruskin Avenue, Kew, Richmond, TW9 4DR
www.south-shields.myby.co.uk/south_shields_history_1.htm Curly's Corner Shop
www.uboat.net U-boats
www.u-boot-archiv.de U-boat Archive Germany

www.ubootwaffe.net u-boat.net 1995 – 2010
www.vsc.co.uk Victory Services Club
www.warsailors.com Norwegian Merchant Marine and Ships 1939-1945
www.warships.web4u.cz
www.en.wikipedia.org/wiki/Defensively_Equipped_Merchant_Ships

Personal Interviews:

Morley, John A. Survivor *SS Peterton*, Hull: Interviewed between July 2004 – January 2010
Midbøe, Dag. Survivor M/V Leiv Eiriksson, Kopervik, Haugesund, Norway: Interviewed February 2004
Baron, Jack. Seaman SS Generton: Interviewed on the 23rd July 2005.

17. ACKNOWLEDGEMENTS

It would not have been possible to tell this story without the help of the following people:

Roger Loughney at Futures Publications, Peggy Meeks, Lynda Tulloch, Janice Levett, Margaret Carlsen, Ian Carlsen, Bill Laybourne, Peter Burns, Isabel McGregor, Ken McGregor, Peter McGregor, Ken Dunn, Dag Midbøe, Lawrence Woodcock, Mike Holdoway, Billy McGee, Horst Bredow at the German U-boat Arkiv, Siri Lawson at www.warsailors.com, Ron Singleton, Gillian Simpson at the Australian Maritime National Museum, Ken near Tilbury, Jack Morley, Clive Winthrop, Bob O'Hara, Robbie Roberts, David Low for German translations, Carl-Eric Carlsen, Jack Baron, Hilary Reynolds at Cullercoats Primary School, Torbjørn Vik Lunde, Vincent Bartley and Haugesund Folkebibliotek.